Praise for *Worn Out by Obedience*

When I first saw the title of this book, I thought, Hey, that's how I feel! I've been following Christ since I was a kid, and there are times I find this lifelong journey to be exhausting. I'm convinced God is sanctifying me—but my sanctification is taking longer than everyone else. And the idea of heading over to Ziklag is a constant temptation. What a breath of fresh air to read Ron's wonderful, story-filled, grace-laden reminder that God is present, working, and wooing even when I don't feel it. Encouraging, relatable, and practical, *Worn Out by Obedience* provided me with much-needed spiritual refreshment and guidance, as I pray it will for you.

BRIAN FISHER
President, Human Coalition

I wish I had read a book like this when I began my ministry over sixty years ago. The author deals with old matters in new ways and introduces topics that may be new to you. You will benefit immensely from studying these pages and putting what you learn into practice.

WARREN W. WIERSBE
Author and former pastor of Moody Church, Chicago

Ron Moore gives us permission to accept reality: everyone feels spiritual fatigue at times. With an engaging mix of Bible stories and easy-to-follow advice, he charts a path to a vibrant, more passionate relationship with Jesus Christ.

MICHAEL ROSS
Bestselling author of *What Your Son Isn't Telling You*

Let's get real! Every follower of Christ wrestles with spiritual fatigue at some point in their lives. Perhaps you are already running on fumes as you face another hour of thankless service in church, battle the same old sin issues, or just try to do the right thing. Based upon King David's Ziklag experience, this no-nonsense book provides the hope and practical help that every weary believer needs to climb out of the valley and to get back on track.

DON LOUGH JR.
Executive Director, Word of Life Fellowship, Inc.,
Schroon Lake, New York

WORN OUT BY OBEDIENCE

RECOVERING FROM SPIRITUAL FATIGUE

RON MOORE

MOODY PUBLISHERS
CHICAGO

All Scripture quotations, unless otherwise indicated, are taken from the Holy Bible, New International Version®, NIV®. Copyright © 1973, 1978, 1984, 2011 by Biblica, Inc.™ Used by permission of Zondervan. All rights reserved worldwide. www.zondervan.com. The "NIV" and "New International Version" are trademarks registered in the United States Patent and Trademark Office by Biblica, Inc.™

Scripture quotations marked ESV are from The Holy Bible, English Standard Version® (ESV®), copyright © 2001 by Crossway, a publishing ministry of Good News Publishers. Used by permission. All rights reserved.

Scripture quotations marked NLT are taken from the Holy Bible, New Living Translation, copyright © 1996, 2004, 2007 by Tyndale House Foundation. Used by permission of Tyndale House Publishers, Inc., Carol Stream, Illinois 60188. All rights reserved.

Scripture quotations marked AMP are taken from The Amplified Bible. Copyright © 1965, 1987 by The Zondervan Corporation. The Amplified New Testament copyright © 1958, 1987 by The Lockman Foundation. Used by permission.

Some names and details have been changed to protect the privacy of individuals.

Edited by Elizabeth Cody Newenhuyse
Interior and cover design: Erik M. Peterson
Author photo: Eliezer Barros Photography
Cover image of man on path © 2017 by Prixel Creative/Lightstock (372836). All rights reserved.
Cover photo of painted wood texture © 2016 by enviromantic/iStock (511864418). All rights reserved.

ISBN: 978-0-8024-1538-7

We hope you enjoy this book from Moody Publishers. Our goal is to provide high-quality, thought-provoking books and products that connect truth to your real needs and challenges. For more information on other books and products written and produced from a biblical perspective, go to www.moodypublishers.com or write to:

Moody Publishers
820 N. La Salle Boulevard
Chicago, IL 60610

1 3 5 7 9 10 8 6 4 2

Printed in the United States of America

To Lori. My wife, inspiration, writing partner,
and the love of my life.

CONTENTS

FOREWORD

Worn Out by Obedience is an honest and convicting book. It is for any of us who call ourselves Christ followers but who, at one point or another along the way, have struggled with spiritual fatigue. Maybe that's where you're at right now. If so, let me assure you you'll find hope in these pages.

As I read the manuscript, it conjured up some not-so-fond memories of my forty-year ministry at Southeast Christian Church. While overall a wonderful experience, there are those memories of incidents I would just as soon forget or relegate to the memory file entitled "too embarrassing to tell." If you don't work in full-time ministry, your experience of being "worn out" might be different than mine, but I bet you'll resonate with those times I experienced fatigue in trying to be obedient to my calling.

Like the time I forgot a wedding. Makes you wonder why the Lord would entrust a wonderful ministry such as Southeast to a buffoon like me. Or the time I was so exhausted before a Sunday evening service that I fell asleep in my office. The worship leader kept adding songs until I finally awakened and stumbled into the sanctuary, disoriented and confused. "I need to get more rest," I later concluded in a blinding flash of the obvious. These incidents tell a story of a young preacher deeply committed to his calling but all too often allowing himself to be overcommitted and exhausted. Nevertheless, I had a wonderful four decades serving at Southeast, though I occasionally struggled with feelings of inadequacy and insufficient time to do all I wanted to do.

Feelings of burnout and spiritual fatigue are not just common to ministers but to all of us. Ron Moore chronicles this situation with uncanny clarity.

After I retired, I began conducting four-day retreats for young senior ministers. Part of the program consists of sharing their ministerial experiences, the high points and the low points. This is great therapy—but it's a little disconcerting to learn how common and pervasive are the feelings of inadequacy, burnout, and depression. A recent email I received from a former retreat attendee makes this point dramatically.

> Dear Bob: I am really struggling right now with an issue I've heard you speak about several times. I am feeling stretched way too thin in my ministry and I'm getting to the point where I'm not doing anything very well. . . . I'm not struggling with any kind of sin or immorality. I'm dealing with feelings of inadequacy and depression. I'm just drained. And my personal walk with Christ seems nearly nonexistent.

These thoughts and feelings are regrettably common among ministers, but they also impact laypeople. I received the following email recently from a layperson serving as a volunteer in a church ministry.

> Dear Bob: I am a strong believer. I am in the Word every day and attend two men's groups. My world is just so noisy that I don't hear His voice very often. My problem is that I am just out of gas. I don't consider my ministry "pure joy" and feel like I have tried to go to Him and find the peace that He promises. But rarely do I experience that peace. I know the problem is in the mirror. . . . not in heaven.

Being "worn out by obedience" is a pervasive, harmful situation that we all experience and one that destroys relationships. It degrades the quality of both our lives and our ministries unless we come to grips with it. How do we do that? In this book, Ron takes a helpful step in that direction by providing an honest assessment of what drags us down and contributes to our sense of spiritual fatigue. More importantly, he reveals how we can improve our personal spiritual condition and help other struggling believers on the journey.

He's earned the right to share this message. For over a quarter-century Ron has served as senior pastor of a multisite megachurch in the Pittsburgh area. Ron holds several advanced degrees while writing four books in addition to this one. Ron and his wife, Lori, have four children and one grandchild. He is involved in enough personal and church commitments to qualify as a candidate for the "burned out" designation. That's why I encourage you to read this book, take notes, and have a serious conversation with yourself and God about where you are at in your walk with Him.

I wish I had had Ron's book when I was just starting in ministry. I know I would have been more effective as a pastor, more loving as a husband, and more engaged as a parent.

BOB RUSSELL
Founding pastor, Southeast Christian Church, Louisville, KY
Author, *After Fifty Years of Ministry*

INTRODUCTION

The Christian life is an exciting journey! Life with Christ transforms our hearts from the inside out and fills us with significance. But even though God provides us with spiritual blessings, life experiences can drag us down. We know that God can be trusted, that His timing is perfect, and that somehow He weaves all things together for our benefit.

But—in the battle, in real time—we become spiritually fatigued, worn down by resisting temptation, exhausted from dealing with difficult people, weary from the emotion of disappointment, tired of waiting. We become worn out by obedience.

The title *Worn Out by Obedience* may seem contradictory. If obeying Christ is the only way to run the Christian race, and if God ultimately blesses obedience, then you might be wondering, "How can one be worn down by the very thing that God rewards?" Although obedience is always the right path to take, that doesn't mean it is the easiest path to take. Easy doesn't always mean right. Right doesn't always mean easy. A life of obedience involves discipline, training, and maneuvering obstacles. Even Jesus faced these challenges during His ministry on earth.

The writer of Hebrews wrote that "During the days of Jesus' life on earth, he offered up prayers and petitions with fervent cries and tears to the one who could save him from death, and he was heard because of his reverent submission. Son though he was, he learned obedience from what he suffered" (Heb. 5:7–8). This may not be a popular message, but there is no way around it. Obedience, even for Jesus, was hard. Certainly it will be hard for us.

Spiritual fatigue is not a character flaw or a condition reserved for the immature or weak Christian. There are stretches of the journey—sometimes long, sometimes short—where we feel like we are just going through the motions, disconnected, distanced, stalled. We have not walked away from Jesus; we're just not moving forward with Him. Greg Hawkins and Sally Parkinson conducted extensive research (more than a quarter of a million people in one thousand churches) to determine the spiritual process in the lives of believers. They discovered that believers are found in one of three stages—"Growing in Christ," "Close to Christ," or "Christ-Centered."[1] Their research also revealed that regardless of which stage believers were in, 92 percent of those surveyed had been stalled at some point in their spiritual journey. Most every believer experiences times of soul weariness. This is an issue we need to be aware of and prepared for. The stalled state leaves a believer vulnerable.

This book is written for followers of Jesus who have grown weary, exhausted from the continued effort to do what's right. I want to address the times when the battle becomes exhausting, when our love for God grows cold, when our passion for Christ has dwindled to smoldering embers.

We will learn that weary stretches are unavoidable . . . but we don't have to remain there. We will seek to understand the danger of apathy toward God and how we can reignite our hearts with a burning passion to follow hard after Him.

This book began with a series of sermons I preached at The Bible Chapel, a church I have pastored for more than twenty-five years. I have delivered many series during my tenure, but few have resonated with our congregation like this one. The guiding text for the series was the story of David's fleeing to Ziklag—enemy territory—when Saul was pursuing him. At our church, "Ziklag" has become a term to describe the stretches of the spiritual journey where a person has become stalled or has strayed. Often I hear people describing a particular time in their life as "being in Ziklag" or "I am praying for my friend. She is in Ziklag." Whether you find yourself in that lonely wilderness or are just feeling worn out (and therefore at risk for a Ziklag experience), my prayer is that this book will resonate with you as it did with our congregation.

PART 1

RUNNING HARD

WORN OUT
BY OBEDIENCE

CHAPTER I

RUNNING ON EMPTY

Leaders in any realm of life, leaders who lead on empty don't lead well and for some time now I've been leading on empty. And so I believe that the best thing for me to do is to step aside. . . . I really need your prayers and I need your support. We've said that this is a church where it's OK to not be okay, and I'm not okay. I'm tired. I'm broken, and I just need some rest.[1] —PETE WILSON

Andrew* loves leading small-group Bible studies. Or rather, he did. Now, after fifteen years of trying to balance a busy career, family life, coaching his children's sports teams, and using his gifts to teach high school students and couples at our church, Andrew is worn down, running on empty. He stepped aside from ministry in order to refill his spiritual tank. In his words: "I was tired of leading and needed to be in a situation where I was being led."

Andrew is attending a new group with his wife, Kathy, and he is beginning to feel God calling him to use his gifts in a more significant way. Right now, he is resisting the urge. Here's how Andrew shared what's going on in his heart.

> *I know that God wants me to step up and lead again, but I have resisted because frankly, I am just tired of the responsibility. I recognize that I am not some all-wise biblical scholar who has all kinds of profound knowledge to share, but God has equipped me with an ability to lead a group of men and women through Bible studies in a way that is relevant and engages the whole group.*
>
> *So, I end up wrestling with the Holy Spirit, which leaves me exhausted . . . and I end up running away and trying to hide. Right now I don't look forward to going to our small group and intentionally don't prepare. I just want to quit . . . but I know that is not the answer.*

> ** Names have been changed*

I believe every Christian can relate to Andrew. I know I can. Whether it is the spiritual fatigue that inevitably comes from using our gifts over a long period of time, the soul weariness from resisting nagging temptations, the exhausting battle to do what's right when disobedience is much more attractive, or the draining circumstances that invade our lives—we become worn out by obedience.

Worn out by obedience. That phrase seems contradictory, doesn't it? Obedience, after all, is the Christian's heartbeat. It's the sincere demonstration of our love for Christ flowing from a heart of gratitude for His work on our behalf. Obedience, made possible by God's empowering presence, digs a deep foundation providing a rock-solid platform from which to launch a life of meaning and purpose. We long to hear, "Well done!" when this life is over, but for now, we are moved by the Spirit's motivating whispers, "Great job!" and "Way to go!"

So how can the very thing that provides meaning and purpose wear us down? How can we tire of that which brings deep satisfaction? How can the blessing of obedience become a dreaded duty? How can following Jesus exhaust us?

Exhilarating and Exhausting

Recently my wife, Lori, and I went hiking in Virginia's Shenandoah National Park. We learned that the "Whiteoak Canyon to Cedar Run Loop" was, according to our National Park app, "among the best hikes—if not the best hike—in Shenandoah." So, we went for it. The trail was a scenic ten-mile loop through dense woods. Along the rocky path, several beautiful waterfalls cascaded into pools where hikers enjoyed a refreshing swim. But this hike was not for those desiring a leisurely walk in the woods. The natural beauty of the trail was accompanied by a challenging ascent. Our legs were feeling the burn and our clothes were soaked with sweat as we climbed for three hours up a narrow path with several stretches of steep steps. After one particularly difficult

Lori looked back at me and said, "Tell me again, why do we think this is fun?"

section, Lori, who was leading the way, looked back at me and said, "Tell me again, why do we think this is fun?" I couldn't think of a good answer.

As soon as we got to the top it was time to head back down.

The descent was another kind of challenge, causing us to use a different set of muscles and forcing us to concentrate on the precarious footing of the steep downward trail.

The trip was exhilarating *and* exhausting! We enjoyed the magnificent scenery *and* wondered if the trail would ever end. When we finally reached our car, took off our packs, and finished what little water was left in our bottles, there was a great sense of accomplishment *and* we were beat.

Like our hiking trip, the spiritual journey is both exhilarating and exhausting. Following Christ is a moment-by-moment, day-by-day experience where we know that the living God is working in and through us. There is nothing more satisfying than that! At the same time, there are long, tiring, seemingly unending stretches when we *don't* feel Him working in and through us, when we question His presence. The right path is not always the easy path. The markings on the trees that indicate you are on the right trail and the signs that warn of challenging terrain often appear side by side.

Here is a sketch that helps me picture what the spiritual journey looks like. The path is challenging, filled with ups and downs. Jesus does not lead us on one smooth trail to heaven. Following the Savior includes high times and low times, remarkable blessings and tremendous challenges, what C. S. Lewis called "troughs."

Notice on the sketch that over

the long haul there is positive progress. This process of spiritual growth is called *sanctification*. When we become Christians the Holy Spirit takes up residence in our hearts, enabling us to do everything God calls us to do. *And* with that enabling power, we have the responsibility to obey, to do what's right when wrong seems easier and, sometimes, more appealing. In his classic work, *The Pursuit of Holiness,* Jerry Bridges uses the analogy of a farmer to explain God's sovereign power and man's responsibility for obedience. He writes:

> *Farming is a joint venture between God and the farmer. The farmer cannot do what God must do, and God will not do what the farmer should do.*
>
> *We can say just as accurately that the pursuit of holiness is a joint venture between God and the Christian. No one can attain any degree of holiness without God working in his life, but just as surely, no one will attain it without effort on his own part. God has made it possible for us to walk in holiness. But He has given us the responsibility of doing the walking; He does not do that for us.*[2]

Together we want to consider our "responsibility of doing the walking." Along with great blessing and times of inexpressible joy, the journey contains a plethora of real and raw emotions, uninvited circumstances, and constant encounters with particular temptations. Obedience is always the right path to take . . . and as we do the walking there are times when obedience is really hard.

- Ask the teenager committed to stay pure while experiencing hormonal explosions.

- Ask the husband and wife who vowed, "for better, for worse" and are now experiencing a long stretch of "worse."
- Ask the couple whose plea for a child continues to go unanswered.
- Ask the single parent trying to honor God while feeling the financial pressure of being the sole provider.
- Ask the young adult who is waiting (and waiting) for God to provide a godly spouse.
- Ask the person whose constant battle with a nagging temptation is wearing them out.
- Ask the person who feels like their sacrificial service goes unnoticed and unappreciated.
- Ask the Christian businessperson determined to do things God's way while others get ahead with their cutthroat, corner-cutting practices.
- Ask the person fighting fear and discouragement while going through another round of treatment.
- Ask the couple serving as caregivers for aging parents.
- Ask the person trudging through the grueling journey of grief.
- Ask the person struggling with an addiction who knows that another relapse is only one weak moment away.
- Ask the parents who have loved and supported their child through years of substance abuse. One mom whose son had yet another relapse shared her heart

with a leader in our church. "She kept telling me last night how tired they are in every possible way. She said, 'This feels like hell on earth.'"

- Ask the person who is spiritually dry.

I was in the sound booth packing up my backpack after church when Sam spotted me and wanted to talk. He said he had been reluctant to go down front after the service and pray with one of our pastors. Sam is a mature believer and active in ministry but, with tears in his eyes, he confessed that he was "spiritually dry." There was no fall into sin or particular circumstance that Sam could point to as the reason for his "trough." But he was feeling disconnected from God and sensing a frightening vulnerability.

Maybe you have shared Sam's experience. On the whole, life is good. You are not worn down from battling a particular temptation nor immersed in a depleting life circumstance. But your soul is dry, and you are frightened by the vulnerability of your spiritual state.

Spiritual fatigue is not reserved for the new or immature believer. It hits us all at various stages of our journey. When the reality of soul weariness is ignored, we slowly slide into dangerous times of spiritual disconnectedness, disappointment, and discouragement. It is during these vulnerable stretches when we are most susceptible to suspend the battle against temptation, lay down our armor, and surrender to sin. As a lion goes after worn-down prey, so Satan charges after the tired believer. We have to recognize the reality of spiritual fatigue, understand the danger, and take the steps to refresh our soul.

A Guide for Our Journey

Does God's Word address soul weariness? Is there a person in Scripture who experienced spiritual fatigue that we can learn from? The answer to both questions is yes.

While we'll consider many passages from Scripture, I want to use a well-known Old Testament king as our primary guide. This king was a warrior, poet, songwriter, and leader. All these roles provided him with a unique mix of experiences ranging from the nightmares of leading men into bloody battles to the tranquility of writing the Twenty-third Psalm. His name was David, and his life was an open book. His prayers and praises, frustrations and questions are journaled in the Psalms. God declared that David was a "man after his own heart" (1 Sam. 13:14), an enviable description used for no other human in the Bible. God's heart and David's heart beat in synchronized rhythm. David was a man of passion, drive, and desire. When his heart was beating with God, he was an unstoppable force. But periods of irregular spiritual heartbeats allowed that same passion to fuel times of blatant sin. He was, at the same time, deeply spiritual and disgustingly human. David was the person we want to be and the person we are.

When David's heart was beating with God, he was an unstoppable force.

We will focus on a particular period when David's soul weariness led him to doubt God and His promises. Worn out by obedience, he made a fateful choice to settle in the land of the enemy.

The Anointing and the Escape

David was a teenager, minding his father's sheep and minding his own business when he was summoned from the fields for a special meeting with the prophet Samuel. Israel's first king, Saul, had disqualified himself by a life of disobedience. While Saul remained the official leader, God prepared Saul's replacement. He sent Samuel to Bethlehem to the house of Jesse to anoint the new king.

Jesse presented seven of his sons to Samuel and God let the prophet know that none was His man. Finally, almost as an afterthought, the baby of the family was called to appear before the prophet. No one was more surprised than David when Samuel said (as I imagine), "You will be the next king of Israel." The prophet "took the horn of oil and anointed him in the presence of his brothers, and from that day on the Spirit of the Lord came powerfully upon David" (1 Sam. 16:13).

From that time, David's life changed dramatically. With God's empowerment, the young man stood up to the Philistine giant, Goliath, who had been taunting Israel's army with an invitation to a one-on-one duel, winner take all. Using his slingshot, David planted a stone into Goliath's big forehead, cut off the giant's head with the giant's sword, and kept both as trophies. Soon David was leading Israel's army in victorious battles. He was given Saul's daughter in marriage and became a kindred spirit with Saul's son Jonathan. Songs were written about David and sung by all the young girls. "Saul has slain his thousands, and David his tens of thousands" (1 Sam. 18:7) were the lyrics set to the popular tunes of the day. David enjoyed rock-star status in everyone's eyes . . . except King Saul.

Saul's jealousy led him to a dark place. He decided to kill David. One day when David was in the king's presence he looked up to see a spear coming toward his head. He ducked just in time. With the spear embedded and vibrating in the wall behind him, David escaped from the man obsessed with jealousy. And David ran from Saul for the next eight-and-a-half years!

Life on the Run

During David's time on the run, the anointing by Samuel became a dull memory; he wondered if he had misunderstood what the prophet told him about being the next king. The fight with Goliath and the victories in battle seemed to be part of another lifetime. David wondered if God's promise would ever come true. David had trusted God, followed God, obeyed God, but after almost a decade of running he became worn out in body and soul.

David convinced himself that one day Saul would kill him. Knowing that the king would not pursue him into enemy territory, David decided to cross the border into Philistia, the land of the enemy. There he gained favor with one of the five Philistine kings. David and his soldiers settled with their families in a little city called Ziklag. In Ziklag, David disengaged from God and lived a life of lies and cover-up.

Ziklag: Short Visits, Extended Stays, Settling In

Sooner or later, every believer experiences spiritual fatigue. Like David, we can become worn out by years of service. We can feel used or unappreciated when our identity is found in serving rather than in the One we serve. We are worn down by harassing temptations that constantly nip at our heels and trip us up. We are overwhelmed by the weight of expectations placed on us by the Christian community and unrealistic expectations we place on ourselves. Life circumstances hit us like a rogue wave and send us tumbling in the sea of disappointment. When we are worn out, Ziklag looks inviting.

The time we spend in Ziklag may last for a few minutes, a few months, or a few years. The short jaunt into enemy territory may be a conversation of regrettable gossip, an outburst of anger, a quick click to a raunchy website, a social media connection that surfaces unhealthy emotions. In these cases, conviction is swift and heavy. Realizing the danger, we quickly turn around and head back home, seeking God's forgiveness and sustaining grace.

Sometimes the stay is much longer. Our spiritual fatigue makes us believe we need a short vacation from God. As a tourist explores the sights of a city, we explore Ziklag's alluring attractions. We fall back into old sinful patterns, ignoring the danger and embracing the sin. The gossip becomes a juicy morsel we continue to enjoy. The relationship with our spouse remains tense. We cross the line of sexual purity. The social media message becomes an ongoing conversation. We choose to remain disconnected from God. Then, one day through a confrontation from a friend, an encounter with God's Word, or an experience that produces a sudden sense of the danger, we pack up and move back to the land of obedience.

Sometimes our Ziklag experience is more than a quick stop or a short visit. Our spiritual weariness leads to relocation. We conclude that the land of obedience is a place of discouragement and disappointment. So we pack up our heart and settle in our personal Ziklag.

The Reality of Soul Weariness

This book is for believers—those whose lives have been transformed by a personal relationship with Jesus Christ; those who are committed to follow hard after Jesus; those who are engaged in the spiritual battle; those who live to make an impact in their generation for Christ. Too many professing Christians stand on the sidelines hardly breaking a sweat, but those in the game spend themselves for the things of eternal significance. They desire to honor God at home, at work, in the classroom, and among their network of friends. With God's strength they fight badgering temptations, use their spiritual gifts to serve God and others, and trust God through the inevitable challenges of life. They live with the weight of expectations—sometimes unreasonably placed on them by others, sometimes burning from an inward desire to move faster and further in their spiritual walk. These serious believers—those in the game— can become worn out.

In my twenty-five years of pastoring a church, I have seen it happen too many times: soul-weary believers drop out of service, leave the church, isolate themselves from caring friends, and settle for a time in Ziklag—dangerously distanced from God. This book is written to address the issue of soul weariness—what it looks like, the dangers it brings, and how, by God's grace, we can recover and resume the great adventure of following hard after Christ.

Recently, Lori and I were out for dinner with another couple when our friends asked if we had heard about the latest pastoral casualty. I recited the long list of well-known pastors who had resigned or been asked to resign from ministry. But the one they had just heard about was a new one. They texted me a YouTube link to a short video where the pastor explained why he was stepping down. He did not mention an affair or inappropriate relationship. There was no mishandling of money or an overbearing personality that had been driving staff from the church. The pastor had not been charged with plagiarizing; nor had he rejected a theological tenet of the faith. He said that he was simply spiritually exhausted.

In a heartfelt message the pastor explained how and why he had started the church a decade earlier. He reported how the church had grown to almost ten thousand people and how he had poured his life into making that happen. But he admitted that while he was busy doing ministry and seeing great progress take place, he had ignored a growing spiritual fatigue. While he was obediently doing the things it takes to grow a church, he did not prioritize important heart issues. He explained,

> Leaders in any realm of life, leaders who lead on empty don't lead well and for some time now I've been leading on empty. And so I believe the best thing for me to do is to step aside. . . .
>
> And now, more than ever before—I really need your prayers and I need your support. We've said that this is a church where it's OK to not be okay, and I'm not okay. I'm tired. I'm broken, and I just need some rest.[3]

Spiritual fatigue is something every believer will experience. Sometimes we run out of gas while serving. Sometimes expectations wear us down. Sometimes disappointments deplete our spiritual drive. It is foolish and dangerous to ignore these spiritual realities. It's okay to admit you're not okay. It's okay to acknowledge that you are running on empty. It's okay to admit that you are tired, broken, vulnerable, and need some rest. But it's not okay to settle for a life in Ziklag.

Through the following chapters we will discover the things that wear us down, the dangers of Ziklag, and God's grace and power to recover from spiritual fatigue. Jesus knew that along the way we would get tired. That's why He said, "Come to me, all you who are weary and burdened, and I will give you rest. Take my yoke upon you and learn from me, for I am gentle and humble in heart, and you will find rest for your souls" (Matt. 11:28–29). Let's take a journey together and find refreshment and rest for our souls.

Jesus knew that along the way we would get tired.

Reflect

1. Andrew described a time when he was running on empty. Describe a time when you experienced this same soul weariness.

2. What were the circumstances that led to your spiritual exhaustion?

3. When David wore down he decided to cross over into enemy territory and settle in Ziklag. When you become weary, where are you tempted to escape? Why do you think "Ziklag" is so attractive to us?

4. Check out the sketch on page 22. Where would you place your present experience on the up-and-down continuum?

5. Read Matthew 11:28–29. Why does Jesus invite us to a place of rest?

Take a moment to tell God about the things that wear you down spiritually. Ask for His wisdom in dealing with these vulnerable times.

CHAPTER 2

WORN OUT BY SERVICE

Let us not become weary in doing good, for at the proper
time we will reap a harvest if we do not give up.
—GALATIANS 6:9

Michael was using the things he did professionally—video, lighting, and editing—to serve in a local community of believers. He found it satisfying to apply the expertise gained from his career to enhance worship and communication. However, Michael shared with me that the leader of the church's technology ministry wasn't always easy to work with. The person was impatient and often seemed upset. Michael felt that many of his suggestions were ignored.

"I began to feel that my hard work was turning into a job, rather than serving the Lord," Michael said. "In addition, I was feeling unappreciated. Eventually, I stepped down. I even became unwilling to go to that church. . . . Discouraged, burned out, and disappointed, I moved on to a different church."

Serving the Lord involves working with people and sometimes those people exhaust us. We can be worn down by those we work with. However, other times it's not the people, but the ministry itself that can make our soul weary. That's what happened to a longtime member of our church.

Over the years Cheryl has been involved in many areas of service. She is currently a member of our missions team and leads groups of women on short-term mission trips to Panama. When Cheryl sensed God's calling to start a special prayer ministry for our missionaries, her initial excitement gave way to fear. She knew that communicating with missionaries for continued prayer requests and relaying these to our church would be extremely time-consuming. And honestly, praying for missionaries, while so important, is not that compelling to many people. As Cheryl put off God's calling, she said, "I was miserable, full of fear and under deep conviction, not to mention very disappointed in myself."

Finally, Cheryl began the special prayer times. However, when the evening of prayer rolled around she admitted to having a "crisis of faith," wondering if anyone would come. "I would be lying if I said that this ministry isn't a heavy burden—because it is. It was especially in the early months. Every month I wanted to quit. . . . I also get discouraged because I focus on the size of the group that comes to pray."

Service can wear out the most mature and passionate believer. Spiritual exhaustion doesn't always come in a pre-packaged, predictable pattern. It can strike in long stretches, days of soul weariness, or short periods when we have a "crisis of faith." Who hasn't experienced a period when service felt more like a job than a joy? Who hasn't felt the spiritual fire fizzle? Using our spiritual gifts can ebb and flow, with times of energy and excitement interspersed with times of fatigue and discouragement. One day you are ready to win the world; the next day you are overwhelmed by the routine things that serving requires.

On two separate occasions I chose to cut short my family vacation to officiate memorial services. Both individuals who had passed away were friends and longtime members of our church. I had promised one of them that even if I were traveling I would return to do their service. I am honored when a person asks, "Will you promise to do my funeral?" and in the emotion of those moments, I have always agreed, feeling that it was inappropriate to discuss the many things that might keep that from happening. In these two instances I had made a promise and needed to keep it.

When I headed back to Pittsburgh, I was frustrated, no, I was angry, that I had to leave my family. Our children, now grown, live in different parts of the country, so cutting the time short was painful. I resented making the promises to officiate the services and became irrationally upset . . . at everyone. Why wasn't another pastor on our staff doing the services? (Several would have gladly officiated them.) Did the elders know the sacrifice I was making? (The elders had placed absolutely no expectation on me to return.) I was irritated one moment and feeling guilty that I was irritated the next. I was worn down from doing what I had promised. I admit it; my self-pity was pitiful, *and* it was real and wearying.

Spent from Serving

Nothing is more satisfying than using the spiritual gifts that God has given you. If you have the gift of leadership, there is deep fulfillment in taking the reins, casting vision, and inspiring people to a meaningful mission. For those with the gift of administration, digging into the details and designing a process to organize information, people, and resources for spiritual impact is rewarding. If God has given the gift of evangelism, you have to share the gospel. You actually choose the middle seat on a plane in order to share Christ with the person to your right and left—before the plane takes off. You lead more people to Christ sitting on the tarmac than others do during their entire lives! These same gifts that bring deep satisfaction can also deliver spiritual fatigue.

In my years of ministry I have watched godly servants crash and burn. I have seen those who served with passion fade off into inactivity or leave the church altogether, bemoaning the fact that they were the only person serious about serving. A person who oversees finances begins to believe that she is the only person in the church who really cares about the budget. ("You people with vision need a reality check!") Those who love to pray are frustrated that more people don't turn out for the prayer service. ("Why are our prayer services so poorly attended? We need a series on prayer!") Those who love to teach children believe that everyone should have that same passion and feel like they are the only ones who really care about the next generation. ("What could be more important than teaching our children? People need to step up and serve in children's ministry!") People with the gift of giving begin to feel like they are carrying the whole financial load. ("We need more teaching on stewardship. Giving is the best barometer of a person's heart!") When busy men and women spend several hours each week preparing to teach an adult class and only a few people show up, discouragement turns into a "what's-the-use?" attitude.

And certainly pastors carry the "I'm the only one who cares" virus. I heard a pastor of an influential church say, "Sometimes I feel like I am the only person in our congregation who cares if the seats in our auditorium are filled on the weekends."

There is one group of servants I would put in a separate category—those who can't say no. Like Will Rogers, who never met a man he didn't like, these servants never met a ministry they didn't feel a need to be involved in. They lead a small group, volunteer with the youth, serve on the hospitality team, and make sure all the Christmas decorations are up the Sunday after Thanksgiving and down the Sunday after Christmas. When there is a service at the church they are there; often the first to arrive and the last to leave. The kids of this "can't say no" group are the ones running around the lobby or sitting on the floor in a hallway doing homework while mom cleans up after teaching a class and leads a "quick" meeting with the curriculum team. The "can't say no" group is filled with faithful servants . . . and prime targets for spiritual fatigue.

> **Whether your ministry is on the stage or behind the scenes, most service takes place with little appreciation.**

One friend told me a story about serving on the adult ministry team at her church. The team oversaw various programs including the Christmas banquet, which at this church was a big deal. She "rashly" agreed to head up the planning and wound up doing way too much and feeling very angry with some team members who bailed on their commitments. She said, "I vividly remember walking into the church office, talking to the church board guy who was sort of the interim leader in the absence of a regular pastor, and bursting into tears. And then I went and experienced some of the same things at our next church!"

Whether your ministry is on the stage or behind the scenes, most service takes place with little appreciation. That lack of encouragement for service, along with the inevitable criticism, can become a heavy load. After a while the very thing God made you to do can suck the satisfaction right out of your heart. Churches across the world are filled with worn-out servants, from the pulpit to the pews.

In the back of the worship center of our church is a steep section of fifteen rows we call the bleachers. Often before a service I take time to greet the people in that section. Some just love to sit in that part of the worship center. They tell me, "These are the best seats in the house!" But many see the bleachers as a place to recover. They tell me that they are new to our church and just need to sit in the back for a while. They explain how deeply involved they were at their former church and how things went south. I can see the weariness in their eyes. In the bleacher seats I have met pastors and pastors' wives who are spiritually exhausted. I have met musicians, former elders, and leaders of large ministries who confessed that they need a break, need to rest and refuel, need to heal. Sadly, many soul-weary believers don't find a place to replenish; they simply check out of church altogether. We find the same situation in the life of King David. He became worn down by significant acts of service and decided to abandon the path of obedience.

What's the Use?

David was a man after God's own heart, blessed with a variety of gifts and empowered by God's Spirit. David was a musician and wrote many of the psalms that Israel sang during their times of worship. Early in his life David used his musical gifts to soothe King Saul, who was tormented by an evil spirit. Whenever the king was in distress, "David would take up his lyre and play. Then relief would come to Saul; he would feel better, and the evil spirit would leave him" (1 Sam. 16:23).

David employed his gift of faith to face the Philistine champion Goliath. For forty days, every morning and evening, the giant had taunted God's people. He invited an Israelite warrior to a battle, mano a mano, winner take all. While Saul's men were "dismayed and terrified" by the offer, David stepped up. Exercising great faith, he stared down Goliath and declared, "You come against me with sword and spear and javelin, but I come against you in the name of the LORD Almighty, the God of the armies of Israel, whom you have defied" (1 Sam. 17:45). With God's strength David bested Goliath, allowing the Israelites to rout the Philistines.

David's leadership gifts were demonstrated in several military victories. He was so successful that Saul gave him a high rank in the army. The promotion "pleased all the troops, and Saul's officers as well" (1 Sam. 18:5). However, David's gifts led to Saul's jealousy and the determination to kill the young leader. No doubt David was confused when his acts of service put him on the run from the resentful king—on the run for eight-and-a-half years!

During those years, David had two opportunities to end Saul's pursuit. The first took place in the Desert of En Gedi, a barren land surrounded by rugged mountains. At one of the many caves that pepper the mountainside, Saul retreated inside to relieve himself. He had no idea that David and his men were hiding in the darkness of the cave. David's men were overjoyed, certain that God had delivered Saul into their hands. David crept up behind Saul, but instead of ending the king's life, David cut off a corner of Saul's robe. David's men were ready to take Saul out and end the chase, but David was determined to serve God and Saul rather than his men. He told the disappointed soldiers, "The LORD forbid that I should do such a thing to my master, the LORD's anointed, or lay my hand on him; for he is the anointed of the LORD." David reprimanded the soldiers and would not let them attack the king. Unaware of the heated debate going on behind him, Saul left the cave and returned safely to his soldiers.

After Saul went a distance, David emerged from the cave and called to him, "Why do you listen when men say, 'David is bent on harming you'? This day you have seen with your own eyes how the LORD delivered you into my hands in the cave." David showed Saul the corner of his robe that had been cut off. Saul wept aloud when he saw that his life had been spared. "You are more righteous than I," he said. "You have treated me well, but I have treated you badly. You have just now told me about the good you did to me; the LORD delivered me into your hands, but you did not kill me" (1 Sam. 24:17–18).

After the exchange, Saul returned home to his palace. But David, certain of future battles with Saul, took his men and returned to the caves in En Gedi. I imagine that the result of this encounter was discouraging. David had faithfully served God by sparing Saul's life but continued to live as a fugitive.

Some time later Saul learned that David was in the Desert of Ziph and resumed the chase. One night David's scouts spotted the location of Saul's camp. Saul and his army were sleeping, the king in the middle with his men circled around him. In the dark of night David and one of his men, Abishai, crept silently into the camp and located the sleeping king with his spear stuck in the ground near his head. Abishai said to David, "Today God has delivered your enemy into your hands. Now let me pin him to the ground with one thrust of the spear; I won't strike him twice" (1 Sam. 26:8). Once again David refused to kill Saul. "As surely as the LORD lives," he said, "the LORD himself will strike him, or his time will come and he will die, or he will go into battle and perish. But the LORD forbid that I should lay a hand on the LORD's anointed" (1 Sam. 26:10–11). David left with Saul's spear and water jug to prove he had been standing over the king.

The next morning David crossed a valley and stood on a hill opposite Saul's camp. This time David cried out to Abner, the commander of Saul's army, who was charged with protecting the king. He showed Abner Saul's spear and water jug, reprimanding the commander for not guarding the king. When Saul saw his spear and jug, he said, "I have sinned. Come back, David my son. Because you considered my life precious today, I will not try to harm you again" (1 Sam. 26:21). But David knew better. While Saul and his men returned home, David and his men went back to their headquarters tucked away in the harsh desert mountains.

Sparing Saul's life on these two occasions were significant acts of service proving David's loyalty. With victory literally one sword thrust away, David refused to kill God's anointed. Scripture does not detail the reaction of David's men after this encounter, but I'm sure there was much grumbling. The men were tired of running, tired of sleeping in caves, and tired of always being on the lookout for Saul's elite soldiers. Twice their leader had refused to end the pursuit. Saul and his men went back to the comforts of home, while David and his men continued their life on the run.

The astounding faith that enabled David to take down a ten-foot giant with a slingshot was waning. After the last incident with Saul, "David thought to himself, 'One of these days I will be destroyed by the hand of Saul. The best thing I can do is to escape to the land of the Philistines'" (1 Sam. 27:1). Can you hear the defeat in David's voice? These two acts of obedience proved to be the tipping point. The calling on David's life, once so clear, was now in a state of confusion. David's passion to serve God escaped his heart like a slow leak, leaving his emotions flat. The promise of God had been beaten down by the disappointment of obedience without the expected rewards.

Can you identify with David? You are committed to serve. You desire to use your gifts. You are committed to fulfill your calling. But today you are tired . . . worn out by the very thing God has called you to do.

Finding Strength in the Lord

Matt is a pastor on our staff who also serves as a chaplain in the United States Army. Recently, Matt was deployed and spent a year in Africa away from his wife and two daughters. God had called him to a great mission, ministering to soldiers, many of whom were heading into combat. But his responsibility at the base in Djibouti, ministry schedule, and the emotional energy spent by being away from his family were wearing on him.

One of Matt's primary responsibilities was to travel to many "outstations" where a smaller number of troops were located. Since he was one of only two chaplains in the area able to travel across the continent, he knew that the Easter season was going to be exhausting. When it was all said and done, Matt preached nine times in five days in seven separate countries! The task of preparing for the messages, handling all the logistics, and coordinating the purpose of the trip with those

"It was at that moment that the Lord reminded me that I could not pull it off, but through Him it would be done."

in command became overwhelming. Matt said he could hardly sleep from worrying about the trip and began to wish it would be canceled.

I was actually getting sick at my stomach wondering how it could be done. It was in that moment that the Lord reminded me that I could not pull it off, but through Him, it would be done. Needless to say, that mission ended up producing the most fruit that I experienced personally while overseas. The turnout and response far surpassed my expectations, and I also got to experience the most exciting moment of my tour during this mission. While out in the Ugandan jungle, as we were beginning to have a campfire Good Friday service, one of the Navy SEAL operators surprised me by pulling out bagpipes and playing "Amazing Grace" for all of us. It brought us to tears.

Using our gifts in service is extremely fulfilling . . . and, at times, exhausting. The preparation, presentation, follow-up, all the behind-the-scenes, thankless parts of ministry can wear out body and soul. Those we serve alongside are sometimes hard to work with. We overcommit and dive in over our heads in ministry obligations. We serve in an area for so long we lose the excitement and become stale. But in our spiritual fatigue God's amazing grace shows up in unexpected ways. Sometimes encouragement that comes in the midst of soul weariness—a song in the night—refocuses our perspective and refills our heart with God's strength. We are replenished for another stretch of the journey. Other times refreshment comes in taking a break from service. At our church, all of our elders can take a sabbatical after three years and must take a sabbatical after six years. We encourage all those who serve to take time off to recharge. The journey is not finished. God has great things for you to do (Eph. 2:10). But you can't serve with an empty tank. Take the time to refuel and soak in God's amazing.

All of us must remember this one thing: Rewards for service don't come from the people you serve. True refreshment is not found in the money you give or the people you teach. You cannot be replenished by serving "on the stage" or "behind the scenes." You can never find in another person what you can only find in Christ. David declared, "Truly my soul finds rest in God" (Ps. 62:1).

Remember Cheryl, who was called to lead a prayer group for missionaries? When she gets discouraged and wants to quit, she remembers, "This is not my ministry. It is the Lord's. He leads it, He carries it, and He moves it along. But when I forget this, I get overwhelmed again, filled with fear, and have another crisis of faith."

So, when you serve, remember who you serve. Humbly present all of your energies, efforts, abilities, and gifts to God—the Audience of One. Use the great gifts God has given you. God promises that "at the proper time we will reap a harvest if we do not give up" (Gal. 6:9).

Reflect

1. List the areas in which you have served over the past five years. What areas have you enjoyed the most? Why?

2. What areas of service seem to wear you down? What are some of the things that make serving in those areas so challenging?

3. I have a friend who says, "When I get tired, everyone else gets stupid." What are your warning signs that spiritual fatigue is around the corner?

4. What do you do to refuel your weary soul?

5. Servants love to serve and often fall into the "Can't Say No" trap. What do you do to guard against overcommitment?

CHAPTER 3

WORN OUT BY EXPECTATIONS

*And a lot is expected of us. A great performance is
expected every time. That's the standard. . . . Not that
we achieve it every time, but we attempt to. When we
don't, that's going to be news. That's a big emotional
investment for every game.*[1] —MIKE KRZYZEWSKI,
HEAD BASKETBALL COACH, DUKE UNIVERSITY

Years ago I would frequently listen to a popular Christian
program aimed to encourage marriage and parenting.
I often turned off the radio after the broadcast feeling like a
complete failure. I remember one particular show that focused
on the topic of family devotions. The fathers being interviewed
explained how their family devos were creative, dynamic,
age-appropriate, and, of course, theologically deep. One father
told how he had recruited other families to join together in
order to construct a life-size cross in the garage—where each
step of construction was perfectly synchronized with the story

of Jesus' death. In his story there were saws, nails, and sandpaper with ten children working in unison while parents took turns explaining the atonement (probably using the original Greek) to their captivated sons and daughters. Seriously?! The program was aimed to help me be a godly father but made me feel like a great failure. I couldn't get my four kids to sit still around a table for a ten-minute Bible lesson and prayer, much less organize a neighborhood devotional workforce!

And poor moms. They were the target audience for this program. Women who had written books about how to be a model mother were interviewed in a beautiful studio reciting well-rehearsed messages. Meanwhile, a worn-out mom, who had been up all night with a sick child, listened to the program as she prepared lunch for her first-grader, cleaned up from breakfast, set out items for dinner, and tried to figure out if she could get all the work for her remote job done during her toddler's naptime. The nature of the program always struck me as curious—a woman *away from her family* promoting a book that taught women *at home with their families* how to be a godly mother. But then, I do struggle with cynicism.

Inside, Outside

Expectations! They hit us from every angle. Some are poured on from the outside, making us feel like we are journeying through life carrying a backpack filled with heavy burdens. Expectations come from parents, family members, teachers, coaches, roommates, employers, employees, work associates, friends, spouses, children, the culture, and the church. Too often we wear ourselves out trying to meet these external demands, burn emotional energy, and become frustrated that these expectations were put on us in the first place.

Other expectations are self-induced. They swell up from within, building pressure on our soul. These internal expectations often grow from the seeds of trying to please a parent or significant person in our life, competition with a sibling, growing

We feel like our actions should be flawless or near flawless— every time.

up in a family where acceptance was performance-based, or being in a church with a performance-based theology. We feel like our actions should be flawless or near flawless—every time. Perfection is an unrealistic pursuit that leaves us spent.

I recall a pastor who had trained under a well-known preacher and leader. After the internship the pastor began his ministry at a church hundreds of miles away from his mentor, but he was haunted by the high-profile leader's influence. In writing a sermon he wondered if his mentor would approve of the content. In preaching a sermon he wondered if his mentor would approve of the message and delivery. When he made a leadership decision it was made in the shadow of his mentor. He was exhausted by self-induced expectations planted in him by a person in his past. Finally, he wrote a letter to his mentor explaining how much he had appreciated the man's investment in his life. Then he added, "I just want you to know I don't need your approval anymore." Such is the power of internal expectations. We are burdened with what those in our past think about what we are doing in the present.

In this chapter we will consider three arenas of expectations. We'll start by considering the expectations placed on us by others. Allowing these to build up delivers us to a spiritual breaking point. Then we'll take a look at the expectations we put on ourselves. These internal pressures can produce independence and turn us away from reliance on God. Finally, we will consider the expectations, often unrealistic, that we place on others. This leaves us perpetually disappointed, and can lead to a disillusionment that damages relationships.

External Pressure: Expectations from the Outside

Christians of all ages are loaded down with expectations. You are expected to choose the right college, be surrounded by the right friends, find the right mate, secure the right job, and have your life mission nailed down before walking across the stage to receive your college degree. You must exercise more, eat healthier, and have meaningful personal devos every day. (Of course, the earlier in the morning the better. Who decided that?)

You are to be a super mom and dad with super kids. Normal doesn't seem to cut it anymore. (Have you ever seen a bumper sticker that said, "My Child Is Average"?) You must make sure your children are picked for the gifted classes, participate in enriching activities, and play on the all-star teams. You, of course, must deliver your kids to programs, parties, and practices, not to mention coaching their teams (which is a good way to make sure your child is on the all-star team). It seems that children raised in Christian families today must trust in Christ by the time they are four years old, or parents begin to panic and wonder if their kids are among the chosen.

You are expected to volunteer in the classroom, deliver the best snacks to soccer games, serve significantly at church, take your wife on date nights, always look your very best for your husband, and together enjoy a vibrant, energetic sex life. At the same time you must put in at least fifty hours a week at work, lead in sales, and be in line for the company's executive team. Then, of course, there are those mundane things like yard work, home updates, car upkeep, doing the laundry, shopping for groceries, repairing leaky toilets, and unclogging the toilet when one of your kids decided to use the whole roll!

The inability to filter these demands through the screen of our personal situation leads to us being worn out.

I admit that those of us who are church leaders often add to the weight. We challenge believers to represent Christ in the workplace, lead early-morning Bible studies, love their spouse sacrificially, be a godly parent raising godly children, attend a weekly small group, and, of course, serve significantly in the church.

None of these expectations are unbiblical. In fact, they are all important for spiritual growth. But no one can possibly do everything at once. The inability to filter these demands through the screen of our personal situation and stage of life leads to being worn out by expectations.

As a pastor I have made the mistake of not helping people realistically assess what they are able and not able to do in their current season of life. Consider, for example, short-term mission trips. I have been greatly impacted by such trips, working with Christians in many parts of the world. I am encouraged by the commitment and faith of these godly men and women, many of whom live in very difficult circumstances. For me these trips provide spiritually stretching and enriching times where I see my smallness and God's bigness. Since these trips have been meaningful to me, I gave the challenge for every teen and adult in our congregation to serve overseas. However, in putting out this call to go on a mission trip, I unintentionally put many people on a guilt trip.

I met one man for lunch during the time of my mission push. His children had been on an overseas ministry trip, but he apologetically told me that he and his wife didn't feel led to go. He said, "Not far from our house is a retired veterans' facility. These heroes get few visitors, so on many Friday nights my wife and I buy ice cream, take it to the vets, and spend time with them." Then he asked, "Are we doing enough?" My emphasis on mission trips made him feel like he was a second-class Christian, even though he and his wife were involved in significant and meaningful service to retired veterans throughout the year. After this conversation, I realized my enthusiasm for all to "go" was putting a burden on many in our congregation.

The reality is that not every believer is able to travel overseas due to health, work situation, finances, or stage of life. Frankly, some just don't feel God leading them to minister in another country. I apologized to our congregation for placing an unrealistic load on their shoulders.

Forty Years of Expectations

When I think of a person in Scripture who lived with the weight of external expectations, I always think of Moses. Moses was a man who walked with God. His spiritual résumé reads like this: "No prophet has risen in Israel like Moses, whom the LORD knew face to face, who did all those signs and wonders the LORD sent him to do in Egypt—to Pharaoh and to all his officials and to his whole land. For no one has ever shown the mighty power or performed the awesome deeds that Moses did in the sight of all Israel" (Deut. 34:10–12). That's impressive! God chose this humble, reluctant leader to deliver His people out of slavery and into the Promised Land. But, due to disobedience, what was meant to be a victorious march into Canaan turned out to be forty years of wandering in the desert.

For four decades the people grumbled. We should return to Egypt, they said—Egypt, the place from which they had been miraculously delivered.

This desperate plea from an exhausted heart makes one wince.

After one such barrage of complaining, Moses was spent. With the people wailing at the entrance to his tent, the leader had an intense conversation with God, beginning with a series of rapid-fire questions.

> He asked the LORD, "Why have you brought this trouble on your servant? What have I done to displease you that you put the burden of all these people on me? Did I conceive all these people? Did I give them birth? Why do you tell me

*to carry them in my arms, as a nurse carries an infant, to
the land you promised on oath to their ancestors? Where
can I get meat for all these people? They keep wailing to
me, 'Give us meat to eat!' I cannot carry all these people by
myself; the burden is too heavy for me. If this is how you
are going to treat me, please go ahead and kill me—if I
have found favor in your eyes—and do not let me face my
own ruin." (Num. 11:11–15)*

Man! Moses didn't hold back his words, did he? He had
reached a breaking point from shouldering the people's expectations. This desperate plea from an exhausted heart makes one
wince. Moses's words to God, "If this is how you are going to
treat me, please go ahead and kill me," arise out of soul weariness.
Forty years of leading Israel and trying to meet their expectations
had taken a toll.

In the last year of their wanderings—shortly before entering
the Promised Land—the people were protesting again. Miriam,
Moses's sister, had just died, and no doubt he was experiencing
the grief of her passing. The people gathered to confront Moses
and Aaron. Emotions ran high as the people spewed accusations:
"Why did you bring the LORD's community into this wilderness,
that we and our livestock should die here? Why did you bring
us up out of Egypt to this terrible place? It has no grain or figs,
grapevines or pomegranates. And there is no water to drink!"
(Num. 20:4–5).

God told Moses to gather the people and speak to a rock,
promising that water would pour out. But Moses was so frustrated and worn down he gathered the people and said, "Listen,

you rebels, must we bring you water out of this rock?" (Num. 20:10). Then, instead of following God's instructions, Moses took his staff, raised his arm, and released his frustration by hitting the rock two times as hard as he could. God provided water from the rock, but Moses's soul-wearied act was costly. God said to Moses and Aaron, "Because you did not trust in me enough to honor me as holy in the sight of the Israelites, you will not bring this community into the land I give them" (Num. 20:12).

This incident took place in the fortieth year of Israel's wanderings! Moses had led Israel to the door of the Promised Land, but years of obediently leading an ungrateful group wore him down. The man whom the Lord knew face to face was not allowed to lead the final stage of the long journey. Later Moses pleaded with God to change His mind, only to hear God say, "That is enough. . . . Do not speak to me anymore about this matter" (Deut. 3:26).

There is a powerful and solemn lesson in Moses's story. Moses was not disqualified from eternal life, but he missed out on God's best. After years of obedience, one rash act, born out of exhaustion, led him to forfeit the opportunity to complete his mission. Expectations from the outside can wear us down and leave us vulnerable. Such are the costly consequences of weariness.

Internal Pressure: Expectations We Put on Ourselves

Not only are expectations thrust on us by others, sometimes they bubble up from within. These demands turn our focus inward, away from God. This internal focus causes us to compare ourselves to others, zero in on our personal failures, and take on unrealistic responsibility for others.

Comparing Ourselves with Others

When I first came to The Bible Chapel we had Sunday evening services that focused on Communion. Prior to distributing the elements, different people would request a song to be sung, read a passage of Scripture, share a short devotional, or pray. And some of those people could really pray! Many prayers sounded like pure poetry interwoven with pertinent Scripture and delivered with moving oration. There was an unspoken expectation that anyone who stood to pray had to bring down the heavens.

Many of my peers would sit silently during the entire service. When I challenged them to participate, they said, "Are you kidding? I would sound like a child just learning to read if I prayed after one of those guys. You're on staff. You get paid to embarrass yourself, but there is no way I am going to pray after those super saints." Ironically, the prayers of some created an internal expectation that stifled the prayers of others.

Too often, churches foster an insidious culture that produces busy people with empty lives.

Wherever we are in our spiritual life, someone else is ahead of us. Sometimes we feel like we're making great strides on our spiritual journey, then we go around the bend to see a throng of people ahead of us and end up feeling like we're at the back of the line. Someone prays more often—and more fervently. Someone serves more regularly and with significant results. Someone gives more—or at least more sacrificially. You feel pretty good when you work in a "date" with your teenage daughter—until you hear about Sam, who has had a breakfast date with his daughter every Tuesday since she was three; and after a theological conversation over egg whites and fresh fruit they work on memorizing the New Testament together. They are halfway through Revelation! (Admit it. People like Sam are irritating.)

As believers we are committed to grow in our journey with Christ and do the things that God has called us to do. But when we compare ourselves with others who always seem to be ahead of the spiritual curve, internal expectations can start to wear us down. Too often, churches foster this insidious culture of expectations that produce busy people with empty lives.

Sin That So Easily Trips Us Up

Christians have a deep longing to follow hard after Christ. We desire to read and study God's Word and put it into practice. We want to remain pure and make the right relationship decisions. We yearn to do marriage God's way. We understand the great gift of children and work to be the best parents we can possibly be. To be an influencer for Christ is the goal of our lives.

Every believer is a new creation transformed by the work of God (2 Cor. 5:17). The Holy Spirit indwells us, providing everything needed for a life of obedience and meaning. However, while the penalty of sin is gone, the propensity to sin remains.

Our sin nature is not eliminated until we pass from death to eternal life. Our position is settled; the rubber-meets-the-road practice of the Christian life is the struggle.

Each of us has certain spiritual weaknesses and vulnerabilities. The writer of Hebrews describes these spiritual liabilities as "sin that so easily trips us up" (Heb. 12:1 NLT). In these areas, temptation is like a low-grade fever. We are constantly exerting spiritual energy to fight off the infection. But when we fail to live out God's purpose in God's power, we understand David's description of guilt: "For day and night your hand was heavy on me; my strength was sapped as in the heat of summer" (Ps. 32:4).

Let's not forget that we have an enemy who is on the prowl like a hungry lion ready to pounce and devour (1 Peter 5:8). Satan is neither sovereign nor omniscient, but he is a student of our behavior. Our battle is against the "rulers . . . authorities . . . powers of this dark world and against the spiritual forces of evil in the heavenly realms" (Eph. 6:12). When we fail to prepare for battle we are dangerously exposed to Satan's attack. He knows exactly when and where to place the lure to divert us from obedience. The expectation to win the battle and the reality of too often losing the battle can become exhausting.

Many of you reading this book are high achievers. You set lofty expectations in every area of your life. You demand much from yourself and from those around you. High achievers face a particular kind of pressure.

Mike Krzyzewski, the legendary "Coach K" and the winningest Division I college basketball coach of all time, is certainly a high achiever. As of this writing, he has led the Duke Blue Devils to the Final Four twelve times and won the NCAA Tournament five times. Krzyzewski understands the pressure of winning.

In a *Sports Illustrated* interview the coach was asked if he ever thought of retiring. He said, "There are moments." The reporter followed up, "When do those moments come?" Krzyzewski responded:

> It's when you get really tired. It's not necessarily after a loss. Sometimes it's before a game, when you have a little harder time getting as emotionally into it as you would like. That happens once or twice a year for me. I think you're not a human being unless you experience a little bit of that. And a lot is expected of us. A great performance is expected every time. That's the standard we've [set]. Not that we achieve it every time, but we attempt to. When we don't, that's going to be news. That's a big emotional investment for every game.[2]

Let's face it: Jesus sets a high standard and expectation for obedience. The spiritual life is an emotional investment where obedience is expected every day. However, in our humanity we don't always depend on the Holy Spirit for His help and strength to accomplish this high calling. Each of us has those sins that can so easily trip us up and when we fall, it's big news. The desire to please God, the inevitable failure, and the emotional investment constitute an ongoing struggle that can wear us down.

Responsibility for Others

Comparing ourselves to others and dealing with the low-grade fever of temptations are not the only internal expectations that wear on us. Many believers carry the weight of the responsibility we feel toward others. Children feel the pressure from parents to have the right relationships with friends, give their best in activities, and make good grades. Moms feel the pressure to "do it all" at home, at work, in relationships—and, for that matter, so do dads. Many of us are caring for aging parents. Church leaders feel responsible for the well-being of their congregations. And on and on.

For the most part this is not unhealthy. Loving relationships influence us in a positive way to honor God in every area of our life. As parents we know that our children are a great gift from God and we desire to provide for them physically, emotionally, and spiritually. As spouses we have biblical responsibilities to serve our husband or wife; and again, it is usually a joy to meet these expectations. Likewise, our job or profession places certain expectations on us.

All this is understandable. However, there are times when the weight of expectations can rest heavy on us and we can feel the urge to shake them off or even escape. And that is when our spiritual weariness can deliver us to a vulnerable place.

King David was a leader, and leaders attract followers, and followers have expectations. During his time on the run, eventually their number grew to six hundred. These men were not exactly the cream of the crop. Scripture says, "All those who were in distress or in debt or discontented gathered around him, and he became their commander" (1 Sam. 22:2). No doubt, managing a group like that was packed with pressure. David was expected to provide for his growing group of rebels, many who had their families with them. One can only imagine the conflicts and challenges David addressed daily with his ragtag team. The weight of responsibility that his men placed on David's shoulders was enormous.

Right around this time David got bad news. He learned that the prophet Samuel was dead. It was Samuel who had traveled to Bethlehem to anoint David as Israel's next king. Not only did David mourn the prophet's death, but also there now was no one to verify that God had chosen him to be Saul's successor. With this disconcerting news rattling in his mind, David and his team of misfits continued to run from Saul (1 Sam. 25:1).

The pressure of expectations wears our emotions thin.

It takes a lot of food and provisions to keep six hundred soldiers on the move. So when the group traveled into the area owned by a man named Nabal, David requested needed supplies from the wealthy landowner. While moving through the land, David's men had never taken any of Nabal's sheep. David assumed that Nabal would be willing to share a small portion of his wealth as a show of gratitude. However, in response to the request, Nabal said, "Who is this David? Who is this son of Jesse? Many servants are breaking away from their masters these days. Why should I take my bread and water and the meat I have slaughtered . . . and give it to men coming from who knows where?" (1 Sam. 25:10–11).

The pressure of expectations wears our emotions thin. That's what happened to David. He allowed an ungenerous man to ignite the short fuse of his weary soul. That can happen when we are spiritually tired, can't it? Frustration and disappointment become exaggerated. Little things that we would normally shrug off become big issues we can't shake. Nabal's slight became David's snare, pushing the weary leader into dangerous overreaction.

David told his men, "'Each of you strap on your sword!' So they did, and David strapped his on as well" (1 Sam. 25:13). Like a man who would take a sledgehammer to kill a fly, David took four hundred armed men to wipe out one man and his household! Thankfully, Nabal's wise wife, Abigail, quickly intervened and averted the bloodshed, something David most certainly would have regretted.

The weight of expectations slanted David's emotions, causing him to lose levelheaded discernment. The same thing can happen to us when we are called to shoulder responsibility for others. In our effort to fix the situation, our frailty is revealed. Soul weariness causes us to say and do things that we later regret.

Whatever God has called us to do, He will give the strength and power to do it. With God's help we can carry the responsibilities He gives us without wearing down.

Expectations We Place on Others

Even though we understand the weight of external and internal expectations, sometimes we place unrealistic expectations on others in our lives. These idealistic standards are impossible to meet, leaving us feeling continually disappointed and leaving those around us confused and frustrated. Let's consider some of the unrealistic expectations we may struggle with at home and church.

Expectations on the Home Front

Your spouse is your life partner. You are deeply in love. You dreamed of doing life together. And while your love continues to grow, while life becomes richer and fuller as children come and the years go by, it is completely unrealistic for you to expect your spouse to meet the deepest longings of your heart. If you continue to harbor those expectations, they will continue to go unmet, and you will live in perennial disappointment, damaging—possibly even destroying—the very relationship from which you seek significance. Your spouse cannot meet the deepest need of your heart. Only God can do that. In their book *Intimate Allies,* Dan Allender and Tremper Longman explain the danger:

It is completely unrealistic for you to expect your spouse to meet the deepest longings of your heart.

> *We make our spouses our saviors when we place them on a pedestal and virtually deify them. This imbues them with powers and qualities they cannot offer because it assumes they have passed beyond their own struggles with sin.*[3]

Later in the book the authors add:

> *Marriage can be a wonderful avenue for intimate relationship when we no longer demand that our marriages restore us to the bliss of Eden.*[4]

The marriage connection is the most satisfying human relationship God offers to man. The one-flesh relationship allows us to be united physically, emotionally, spiritually, and missionally. But a spouse cannot offer what can only come from God. When our deepest longing is met in Christ alone, then we will experience true satisfaction in our marriage.

Just as our deepest longing must be met in Christ in the context of marriage, the same applies in the context of parenting. Moms and dads cannot place unrealistic expectations on their children. Our sons and daughters are unique creations gifted by God. We cannot expect them to do what God did not make them to do. Paul is clear that fathers (and mothers) should not "exasperate your children; instead, bring them up in the training and instruction of the Lord" (Eph. 6:4). Although there are many things we can do to provoke our children to anger, unrealistic expectations open the door to frustration and discouragement. When our deepest longing is met by the Lord, we can find our significance in Christ alone and show our children how to find their significance in Him as well.

Expectations from the Church

How many Christians have checked out of church because certain people didn't meet their expectations? A pastor, an elder, a person in their small group let them down in some form or fashion. How many people have been hurt by another believer and never gotten over it? How many believers have left the entire community because of one person's slight?

What a shame!

When we place our faith in another person, disappointment is inevitable. Every person is human, disgustingly so! Everyone is working through the issues of life, just like us. All are dealing with entangling sin and challenging life circumstances. But checking out of church is not an option. Scripture is clear: "And let us consider how we may spur one another on toward love and good deeds, not giving up meeting together, as some are in the habit of doing, but encouraging one another—and all the more as you see the Day approaching" (Heb. 10:24–25). We can't allow ourselves to be exhausted and leave the community of faith because of unmet expectations.

No More Spiritual Supermen

I have pastored a small church, medium-sized church, large church, and a multisite church—all at the same place. When our church was small I visited every newcomer in their home (because one of the elders said that was "essential if the church is to grow"), did hospital visitation, officiated the funerals and weddings (and all the premarital preparation), led a growing staff, worked with the elders, served on ministry teams, edited the monthly newsletter, taught the new members class, and was determined to deliver a well-studied, well-crafted sermon that was true to the Word, theologically deep, and very practical (the well-crafted, well-delivered sermon thing worked out sometimes better than others). As our church and staff grew I was able to delegate many of these responsibilities and focus on the areas where God has gifted me. Honestly, delegating these responsibilities was one thing; letting go of the internal expectations was another.

I will never forget receiving the call that Jim had passed away. Guilt blanketed me. Jim was a godly member and had served as a gifted teacher in our adult classes for many years. He had been ill for several weeks and I had not visited him. When I called to offer my condolences to Jim's wife, Marlyn, she graciously told me that another member of our staff, who had responsibility for the area where Jim served, would be doing the funeral. Another blanket of guilt settled in.

Jim was a godly member of our church. He had been ill for several weeks and I had not visited him.

When my wife, Lori, and I went to the funeral home for the viewing, I had convinced myself that the family would be upset with me. Marlyn was the first person I saw. She walked over to me and said, "I want to thank you for your leadership at our church. During the time Jim was ill so many people came to visit him and prayed with us. We have more food at home than we know what to do with. The staff has been so kind in helping us plan the services. You have a lot of responsibility and can't be everywhere. But thank you for leading a church that can minister to many people." Words could not express my appreciation and relief. God used Marlyn to help me deal realistically with unrealistic expectations.

As long as we are alive expectations will surround us. The feeling that we have to be a spiritual superman or superwoman will exhaust us. When we try to satisfy our soul by pleasing other people, maintaining an impossible standard, or trying to find

WORN OUT BY EXPECTATIONS

fulfillment in a person struggling with sin just as we are, our life will be filled with perpetual disenchantment. But, thankfully, our trust is not in others or ourselves. Spiritual strength comes from keeping our trust in God alone. His promise to us is clear: "those who hope in me will not be disappointed" (Isa. 49:23).

Reflect

1. What are some of the expectations you place on yourself as a follower of Jesus? How do you feel when you fail to meet these standards?

2. What are some of the expectations you place on your spouse (if married)? Do you believe these expectations are realistic?

3. In Ephesians 6:4, Paul warns fathers (and mothers) to not "exasperate your children." In Colossians 3:21, he instructs parents to not "embitter your children, or they will become discouraged." What are some of the expectations you place on your children? Do you believe these expectations could exasperate or embitter them?

4. What are some of the expectations you feel the church places on believers? Do you believe these expectations are in line with Scripture?

5. What steps can you take to deal with the internal and external expectations that wear you down?

CHAPTER 4

WORN OUT BY DISAPPOINTMENT

*Long trials are in danger of tiring the faith and patience
even of very good men.* —MATTHEW HENRY

graduated from seminary with high expectations. After four
years of study and a master's of theology degree in hand,
Lori and I couldn't wait to get started in church ministry. We
were ready and willing to go to any area of the country and take
any pastoral staff position. I sent out résumés from sea to shining
sea. I got a ton of responses, and all could be summarized in
four words: "Thanks, but no thanks."

After a while my high expectations crashed into a deep disappointment. After four months of no leads, I took a teaching
and coaching job at a public school. Teaching and coaching . . .
the very thing I had done *before* four years of seminary. Praying and waiting, making follow-up phone calls and waiting,
sending résumés and waiting, completing questionnaires and
waiting. I was disappointed . . . and worn out.

"I Have Been Patient for Eighteen Years Now"

Disappointment is no stranger to those who follow Jesus. All of us struggle with spiritual frustration and, at times, disillusionment. With God's help we do our best to live with and work through unanswered prayers and uninvited trials. But the disappointment is real, and it makes our soul weary. Eighteenth-century pastor and writer Matthew Henry said it this way: "Long trials are in danger of tiring the faith and patience even of very good men."[1] Job was more straightforward. In response to his great disappointment and loss, he said, "Surely, God, you have worn me out . . ." (Job 16:7).

Ava responded to a blog I had written about prayer with real and raw emotions. She explained, in no uncertain terms, that she was tired of hearing that . . . stuff. Later she sent me an email to explain her frustration.

> *I want to apologize for a very inappropriate post that I made on your Facebook a few weeks ago. I remember after my husband left me eighteen years ago that I asked God to give me patience and I am angry that he answered my prayer. I have been patient for eighteen years now. I have been struggling with anger and my faith.*

Ava is not alone in her struggles. Sooner or later, disappointment hits every believer. Many of you reading this book can well understand Ava's emotions and you may be blaming God for your disappointment. You have been waiting . . . and trusting . . . but it seems God has put your heart on hold.

Some of you have just heard the piercing words, "This relationship isn't working out" or "I don't love you anymore." Some of you have been hit with illness that showed up unexpectedly like a rogue wave and your life is beginning to tumble under the weight of uncertainty. Death—always uninvited—has barged into your life and cut a hole in your soul, leaving you gasping for air and longing to feel "normal" again. Some of you have experienced the death of a dream, having come to grips with the reality that something you've longed for is not going to happen. Some of you are worn out from praying for a loved one to come to Christ. Some of you are working through the stinging betrayal of a person you thought to be a good friend. In this chapter let's consider several disappointing experiences that wear us down—and learn how God meets us in our disappointments.

"I Am So Tired of This": Worn Out by Illness

Bill never lost his love to wax eloquent about the Steelers, the Pirates, or politics. And he never lost his sense of humor, even when he knew he had only a couple days to live. I don't do a lot of hospital visitation since that is the focus of others on our staff, so when I visited Bill during his last days in home hospice care, he said, "Oh, no! You're here. It must be bad!"

Long before Bill lost his life, he lost his health. The struggles began when Bill was diagnosed with diabetes at twenty-nine years old. Seven years later he had a heart attack. Through the years, Bill underwent open-heart surgery, suffered kidney failure, had a kidney/pancreas transplant, and then another kidney transplant. His leg was amputated and he lost muscle use for a time due to medication. Bill was in and out of the hospital more times than he cared to count. Through it all he remained upbeat, kept his sense of humor, and clung to the supernatural strength that only God can give. But . . . sometimes in quiet moments, Bill said, "I am so tired of all this."

Few people can relate to all of Bill's struggles, but many can relate to some of them. You understand the anxiety of waiting for the tests to come back and the sinking feeling/heaviness of hearing the results. You have heard the words, "The cancer is back." You know the spiritual weariness of trusting God through surgery and the slow days of recovery. You know the dread of radiation or another round of chemo. For some of you there is no more treatment available. You simply wait as the degenerative disease takes its toll. Perhaps your illness is not life-threatening but involves chronic, sometimes debilitating pain. You have tried everything there is to try, but nothing has worked. You are learning to live with the "new normal," and you are soul weary.

Psalm 38 is a prayer of David during a time of illness. I am sure that many of you can echo David's anguish as he cried out to God,

> *My back is filled with searing pain; there is no health in my body. I am feeble and utterly crushed; I groan in anguish of heart. All my longings lie open before you, Lord; my sighing is not hidden from you. My heart pounds, my strength fails me, even the light has gone from my eyes. . . . For I am about to fall, and my pain is ever with me. (Ps. 38:7–10, 17)*

Illness does more than drain the light from our eyes; it drains the energy from our soul. You can hear the spiritual exhaustion in David's words: "I groan in anguish of heart." But

David knew that even in his spiritual fatigue, help could only be found in the Lord. In the midst of his weariness and pain he did not turn from the only One who could deliver him. David continued his prayer with confidence, "LORD, I wait for you; you will answer, Lord my God. . . . LORD, do not forsake me; do not be far from me, my God. Come quickly to help me, my Lord and my Savior" (Ps. 38:15, 21–22).

The apostle Paul knew what it was like to live with a physical ailment as well. On three separate occasions he pleaded with God to take away his "thorn in the flesh." God did not remove the weakness but assured Paul of His strength. God said, "'My grace is sufficient for you, for my power is made perfect in weakness.' Therefore I will boast all the more gladly about my weaknesses, so that Christ's power may rest on me" (2 Cor. 12:9). God's grace is always sufficient. He will give us everything we need to do what He is calling us to do.

I recently met with a Christian business leader in Pittsburgh. For years he has led a weekly Bible study that started in his office, then grew to the company boardroom, and finally expanded to a large church. This man has made a tremendous impact for Christ in the business world. When I met with him, he had just been diagnosed with Parkinson's disease. I said, "I am so sorry. You must be going through a difficult time." He said, "I am trying to discover what my new normal is health-wise. But my focus is how I will honor Christ in this illness. The Lord has given me something to manage for His glory." This man knew that even though the disease would weaken him, his focus was to allow Christ to use his illness for eternal purposes.

"Please Pray for Us": Worn Out by Relationships

After each weekend service we invite people up front to pray with our pastors and elders. The majority of those who come desire either prayer for an illness or a relationship. Many couples will come up after a service and simply say, "Please pray for us. Our marriage is going through a challenging time." Others, sadly, come alone and tearfully tell us that their husband or wife is leaving the relationship. Recently a member of our congregation brought up a friend who told me through tears that her husband of more than twenty-five years was leaving. She felt abandoned and afraid.

For those in difficult marriage situations, we always offer marriage counseling, and by God's grace many relationships are restored. But I have to tell you: it is a helpless feeling to watch a person working to revive a relationship with a partner who, for whatever reason, wants out. Only those of you who have fought for your marriage truly understand the spiritual exhaustion that takes over the soul.

By God's grace and the love of a patient wife I have not personally experienced the exhaustion of a painful relationship. But I have spoken with many who have. The rejection, loss, and hurt of a broken marriage sap the strength of the godliest Christ follower. It is said that divorce is worse than death. Death is painful but final, and the bereaved enters the process of grief. Divorce is painful and ongoing as the person who caused the pain continues to show up in your life. The person who fought to keep the marriage together is left in a vulnerable position. Too often the happiness they desire is found in an unhealthy rebound that promises more pain in the future.

If you are worn out by a failed relationship, I encourage you to find a group of people who will walk with you through a process of healing. Our church, like many churches, offers a ministry called DivorceCare. Those who understand the pain of a failed marriage and the vulnerability of recovery lead this ministry. DivorceCare is centered in God's Word and depends on Him to heal your heart before you give it away to another person. Soul weariness delivers dangerous decisions, as we will see in subsequent chapters. Go to divorcecare.org to find a group in your area that is grounded in God's Word. This support will give you the help you need to recover in a healthy way.

Mary had been dating Aaron for more than a year when she became a Christian. At first there was no drastic change in their relationship, but after two years Mary became convicted about being with Aaron, who had not made a commitment to Christ. But Mary was desperately in love and wanted a future with Aaron. So she convinced him to go to church and he even attended the young adult group with her. However, after a while she realized that he was only going to please her. Mary explained her struggle:

> *I knew I needed my husband to be my spiritual leader, and I recognized that Aaron wasn't there, but he said he was a Christian so I told myself it was okay and he just needed more time. Slowly the conviction grew stronger and stronger. For the next eighteen months, I wrestled with God over what to do. I prayed a lot about it. My prayer time was consumed with me pleading with God to change Aaron and to make him into the godly man I wanted him to be. I talked to my friends about it, to my*

pastors. I spoke to anyone who would listen, just hoping that someone would give me a glimpse of hope that God would change him.

As Mary grew in her walk with the Lord, He continued to speak to her about being unequally yoked. Still very much in love with Aaron, but convinced of God's leading, Mary ended the relationship. She said that it "was the hardest thing I have ever done." But she also says that God used that situation to grow and stretch her in ways that would never have been possible had she not obeyed God's will for her.

Obedience is not always followed by an immediate blessing.

Obedience is hard. It involves making difficult decisions that we don't want to make. And obedience is not always followed by an immediate blessing. Mary followed God's will and is still waiting for God's man. She said:

More than three years later, the hardest part of this whole situation is the continuing obedience and trust I have to exhibit each day. Foolishly, I imagined that after ending things with Aaron, God would bless me by quickly bringing my husband into my life. That's not been the case here. I struggle with that trust all the time, but I have never regretted ending the relationship because I know that's what God was calling me to do.

"How Long, O Lord?"

David knew what it was like to wait on God. He understood what it felt like to pray and pray and wait and wait. At one point he confessed, "I am worn out calling for help; my throat is parched. My eyes fail, looking for my God" (Ps. 69:3). In Psalm 13, his petition is more to the point.

> *How long, Lord? Will you forget me forever? How long will you hide your face from me? How long must I wrestle with my thoughts and day after day have sorrow in my heart? How long will my enemy triumph over me?*
> *(Ps. 13:1–2)*

We don't know the circumstances that caused David to question God's care and presence with him. It could have been during his years of running from Saul, but the text is not specific. This we know: David was feeling physically and spiritually exhausted. He holds nothing back in his prayer. I encourage you to do the same. Let your requests be known to God. Tell Him what is on your heart. He knows your struggles, frustrations, and disappointments. I believe one of the reasons that God called David a man after His own heart was David's transparency. David held nothing back. And . . . David always came back to a confidence in the person of God.

David begins his prayer with a series of emotional, heartfelt cries and questions. As he concludes you can almost hear him sigh, close his eyes, and confess,

> *But I trust in your unfailing love; my heart rejoices in your salvation. I will sing the Lord's praise, for he has been good to me. (Ps. 13:5–6)*

Obedient waiting is hard. It may come with cries of, "How long, O LORD!" But let your cries end in a calm confession. His love is unfailing. He has made you His child. You can trust Him—even as you wait.

When It's Not Going to Happen: The Death of a Dream

The death of a dream comes on the day you realize something you deeply desire is not going to happen. You hold the rejection letter from the college you have dreamed of attending since childhood. The girl who stole your heart has chosen another man; they just announced their wedding date. The marriage you fought for is over; he is gone and not coming back. The position you worked and sacrificed for is not going to happen; you have been passed over again. The retirement you dreamed of can never be; the funds aren't there and you will have to accept a more frugal lifestyle just to make ends meet.

She finally asked her husband to stop praying, "Lord, please give us a child," because she couldn't stand to hear it anymore.

Some reading this desperately want a child, but to this point the Lord has not blessed you with a son or daughter, and time is running out. Like Hannah in the Old Testament you are "downhearted" and "deeply troubled." You pour out your soul to God because of your "great anguish and grief" (1 Sam. 1:8, 15–16). Lori and I have a friend who prayed many years for a child. She said that she got sick of praying the same prayer over and over again and finally asked her husband to stop praying, "Lord, please give us a child," because she couldn't stand to hear it anymore. She was worn out from praying.

You may be worn out by praying, and disappointed that your pleas did not result in what you wanted. A renewed trust in God can move you from the dream you had to God's work in your life today. God may not always give you everything you want, but He can satisfy your soul with the great blessing He has already given you.

When the Storm Hits: Worn Out by the "Whys"

When I was nineteen years old I experienced a disappointment trifecta. The college where I played baseball dropped its program. I was without a scholarship, without a place to play, and had to leave a strong network of friends to transfer to another college. That spring a heavy rain hit my hometown in Oklahoma and my car (a 1975 red Chevrolet Malibu Classic—sweet car!) was totaled in a flood. Then the storm really hit.

In March my dad went in for what we thought was a routine surgery, but when the surgeons entered the waiting room to speak to us afterward, the look on their faces conveyed anything but routine. They had found advanced cancer and later, as my family crowded in a small conference room, the doctor told us that my dad had at most six months to live. So we began to pray and trust God to heal him, confident that our prayers would be answered. When I was home from college that summer, there were many nights when my dad couldn't sleep and suffered from the pain. He would ask my mom and me to pray for him. I remember dragging myself out of bed and praying words of comfort with my mouth while asking "why" questions with my heart. My dad wasted away during the next months and died with his family gathered around him in a stark hospital room. My dad knew Jesus and taught me how to live for Christ. By his strong example I saw how to die in Christ as well.

After all these years I still don't know all the reasons for the perfect storm during that time in my life. Maybe it was to put baseball in proper perspective. I went on to play at another college, but the game was not as important as it once had been. Maybe it was to show me how temporary material things are. Maybe it was to show me how a strong believer lives through an illness and faces death. Certainly, there were many lessons I learned. But the biggest one was this: God is still good even when He doesn't answer all our "whys." He is still God and still good in the midst of illness, deep disappointments, difficult relationships, loss of loved ones, and death of dreams. It may feel like God is wearing you down, but the opposite is true. He is building you up, preparing you today for what He has for you tomorrow.

For everyone worn out by disappointment, take courage and find confidence in these words from the Old Testament prophet Isaiah.

> *Why do you complain, Jacob? Why do you say, Israel, "My way is hidden from the LORD; my cause is disregarded by my God"? Do you not know? Have you not heard? The LORD is the everlasting God, the Creator of the ends of the earth. He will not grow tired or weary, and his understanding no one can fathom. He gives strength*

to the weary and increases the power of the weak. Even youths grow tired and weary, and young men stumble and fall; but those who hope in the LORD will renew their strength. They will soar on wings like eagles; they will run and not grow weary, they will walk and not be faint. (Isa. 40:27–31)

God Never Wastes Our Time

God never wastes our time; He never wastes our waiting. He uses every disappointment to shape us into the person He desires us to be. I know it is hard to believe that . . .

> . . . as you are trying to make ends meet between jobs.
>
> . . . as you wait on God to bring the right mate into your life.
>
> . . . as you recover from another round of chemo.
>
> . . . as you live in the consequences of your sin.
>
> . . . as you go through another day with a broken heart over your grown child.
>
> . . . as you accept the death of your dream.
>
> . . . as it feels that your life has been placed on hold.

But the sovereign, all-powerful God never wastes your time.

Remember that teaching job I took after seminary? I stayed at that school for four-and-a-half years! At times I wondered if I had wasted four years of my life in seminary. I moved from high expectations to deep disappointment to a resolve that for some reason a career in education was what God had for me.

back to school and earned a master's of education en

becoming a principal and eventually a superintendent. Finally, God opened the door for me to come to Pittsburgh and join the staff of the church I have served at for more than twenty-five years. I can tell you from personal experience that waiting is hard—but worth it. In that Texas school experience, God taught me that He is God and I am not, that His timing is perfect, and that He had many things for me to learn that were not part of the seminary curriculum. Looking back, I thank God for His gracious work in my life during the time between seminary and ministry in Pittsburgh.

God's ways are not our ways, and His schedule is seldom synced with the calendar on our smartphones. But you can be sure of this: God is not wasting your time. He loves you with an unconditional love. He has given you an inheritance that can never perish, spoil, or fade

God is using today to prepare you for tomorrow.

(1 Peter 1:4). He has purchased you with the precious blood of His Son. He has eternally invested in you! He is using today to prepare you for tomorrow. You can trust Him. God has great things in store for you! And He will show you what they are . . . in His perfect time.

Reflect

1. God told Paul, "My grace is sufficient for you, for my power is made perfect in weakness." Can you identify with Paul's struggle?

2. Obedience is not always followed by immediate blessings. Why do you believe God does not always bless our obedience instantly?

3. Each of us experiences the death of a dream in some area of our life. How are you responding to a longing that continues to be unmet?

4. God never wastes our time! Describe a time when you felt like your life was on hold, but looking back you now see how God used that time to teach you valuable lessons.

PART 2

RUNNING AWAY

THE DANGERS OF SPIRITUAL FATIGUE

CHAPTER 5

MY OWN WORST COUNSELOR

*I felt totally, absolutely alone. And I
probably was alone because I pretty much
had abandoned God.*[1] —DAVID BOWIE

Are you in a life situation that is testing your faith and
trying your patience? Is a lingering illness, stalled career,
or difficult relationship wearing you out? The writer of Proverbs
13:12 says, "Hope deferred makes the heart sick." The Hebrew
word for "deferred" means to "draw out" or "drag on." When
our hopes and dreams are drawn out or keep dragging on without being fulfilled, the result is heart sickness or heart weakness.
Our deferred hope may be the result of service fatigue, the load
of expectations, or life situations that leave us disappointed
and discouraged. Regardless of the cause, the result is the soul
weariness we've been considering.

And . . . this very weariness can place our souls at risk.

We'll see in this chapter that a weary soul, left unchecked, causes us to turn inward and begin the process of taking matters into our own hands. Spiritual fatigue often pushes us to counsel ourselves regarding what is best, irrespective of God's promises and instruction. That's what happened to David and he will be our focus. But let's start with an incident etched on the minds of many Americans.

Roger Boisjoly had a serious concern. The engineer, employed by Morton Thiolkol, the company that made boosters for the Space Shuttle *Challenger*, believed that if the weather was too cold, the seals that connected sections of the shuttle's huge rocket booster could fail. Boisjoly was part of a task force commissioned to examine the effect of cold on the boosters. According to later investigations, their efforts had been mired in paperwork, delays, and a rush to launch the shuttle. Boisjoly's apprehensions were made clear in a memo to his bosses: "The result could be a catastrophe of the highest order, loss of human life."[2]

The night before *Challenger*'s liftoff, the temperature at the Kennedy Space Center dipped to below freezing. The cold was unusual for Florida and unprecedented for a shuttle launching. However, the pleading to postpone the flight was ignored. Seventy-three seconds after launching, the shuttle exploded killing its seven crew members. I am sure most everyone reading this has that terrible scene of the shuttle bursting into flames imprinted on their mind. Perhaps, like me, you saw it happen in real time on January 28, 1986. No doubt, you have watched the incident on anniversary remembrances or on a YouTube video.

Investigations following the explosion found that there was much blame to go around. Certainly there were many complex factors involved in the launch. There was much pressure to get the shuttle in the air. But at the end of day wise counsel was disregarded and legitimate concerns were ignored—ending in a terrible disaster.

The Only Voice We Listen To

On any given day, under a particular set of circumstances, each of us can enter the dangerous mode of self-counsel. During these times we internalize our thoughts and feelings, refusing to listen to any voice but our own. When we really want something we convince ourselves that we can't live without it. When we don't want something we persuade

Self-counsel elevates personal cravings while ignoring possible consequences.

ourselves we can't live with it. Self-counsel leads us down a path that best matches our feelings and desires at the moment. It elevates personal cravings while ignoring possible consequences.

In my years as a pastor I have had many men and women sit in my office and with a straight face tell me that their extramarital affair was divinely ordained. They proclaimed with shocking confidence, "My marriage was a mess, and God brought this new person into my life. I have never been happier! And I know God wants me to be happy."

"Help me understand," I want to respond. "You are saying that the same God who says to keep far from the path of an adulterer, the same God who says that the adulteress preys on your very life, the same God who says that a person who commits adultery lacks judgment—that same God changed His standards just for you? God blessed you with adultery?" Sure, it's ridiculous . . . unless you are engaged in self-counsel.

Self-counsel will lead you away from God to places of irrationality, immorality, dishonesty, debt, addiction, and spiritual bankruptcy. You are your own worst counselor.

"I Am in the Midst of Lions"

David was worn down from the years of running. At one point he had declared, "The LORD is my strength and my shield; my heart trusts in him, and he helps me. My heart leaps for joy, and with my song I praise him" (Ps. 28:7). David described God as his "rock of refuge" (Ps. 31:2), his "hiding place" where he found protection in times of trouble (Ps. 32:7). But his years on the run dulled David's spiritual senses. The long days and lonely nights were wearing him down.

David wrote several psalms while being pursued by Saul. Psalm 57 was written when David had "fled from Saul into the cave." As you read the psalm, imagine David sitting in the recesses of a dark cave near a small flickering fire. He is alone and feels like he is in the middle of a "disaster." He describes his enemies as "lions" and "ravenous beasts." He is "bowed down in distress," fearful, and tired of running. This is a prayer of desperate need. David has not forsaken God, but as you read through this psalm you can hear his discouragement and exhaustion.

Psalm 57

Of David. A *miktam*. When he had fled from Saul into the cave.

Have mercy on me, my God, have mercy on me,
for in you I take refuge.
I will take refuge in the shadow of your wings
until the disaster has passed.
I cry out to God Most High,
to God, who vindicates me.
He sends from heaven and saves me,
rebuking those who hotly pursue me—
God sends forth his love and his faithfulness.
I am in the midst of lions;
I am forced to dwell among ravenous beasts—
men whose teeth are spears and arrows,
whose tongues are sharp swords.
Be exalted, O God, above the heavens;
let your glory be over all the earth.
They spread a net for my feet—
I was bowed down in distress.
They dug a pit in my path—
but they have fallen into it themselves.
My heart, O God, is steadfast,
my heart is steadfast;
I will sing and make music.
Awake, my soul!
Awake, harp and lyre!

I will awaken the dawn.
I will praise you, Lord, among the nations;
I will sing of you among the peoples.
For great is your love, reaching to the heavens;
your faithfulness reaches to the skies.
Be exalted, O God, above the heavens;
let your glory be over all the earth.

Can you hear David's inner struggle? His situation was desperate. Are you in a similar place?

- You feel like you are the only one fighting for your marriage and are tired of fighting alone.
- Your tendency to be a people-pleaser has left you exhausted from overcommitment.
- Your silent battle with same-sex attraction has left you weary and isolated.
- An addiction has you hiding in the recesses of your life.
- Worry has settled in your heart, leaving a paralyzing fear.
- Financial struggles have you pinned down under a pile of debt.
- The pressures at work are keeping you awake at night, robbing you of hours of needed sleep.
- Your devastating situation has you questioning God's love, even His presence.
- A shattered relationship has left you deserted, alone with a broken heart.

Many situations wear us out and cause us to feel alone. We begin to think that no one else cares; no one else is concerned. Our internal turmoil begins to override what

Our internal turmoil begins to override what we know about God.

we know to be true about God. That's what happened to David and led him to take matters into his own hands.

David feared Saul would ultimately overpower him. He was bowed down in distress, pinned down in a personal prison, engulfed with the despair of loneliness. He became convinced that no one was concerned for him and no one cared whether he lived or died. David decided that it was time to take action.

> *But David thought to himself, "One of these days I will be destroyed by the hand of Saul. The best thing I can do is to escape to the land of the Philistines. Then Saul will give up searching for me anywhere in Israel, and I will slip out of his hand." (1 Sam. 27:1)*

Long trials exhaust the faith and patience of godly men and women, even those whose hearts beat with God. Samuel's anointing oil had lost its fragrance. The power David felt when he went up against Goliath was a distant memory. David could hardly remember the tune of songs the young maidens sang about him when he was the young hero.

During his time on the run David had tried to live in obedience. Twice he had a chance to kill Saul and put an end to the king's jealous pursuit, but each time David refused to kill the king . . . against the urging of his soldiers. Each time Saul went home, and David remained on the run.

David began to doubt God's promise. Perhaps he misunderstood Samuel's words about being the next king of Israel. Did God change His mind? David's self-counsel led to an unhealthy conclusion and a dangerous decision. He convinced himself that sooner or later Saul's soldiers would kill him, so he decided to evade the impending threat by escaping to the land of the enemy.

The Downward Spiral of Self-Counsel

Self-counsel is a solo exercise in which I rationalize my actions and always get my way. In the process I set aside God's promises and insert my plans based on how I feel at the moment. Self-counsel ultimately leads to self-deception. That's what happened to David—but he's not the only person in Scripture to engage in the downward spiral. Let's begin at the beginning . . .

Believing the Lies

Self-counsel began in the garden. Adam and Eve had everything they would ever need, everything they could ever want. Surrounded by unimaginable blessing, they were given only one prohibition—"You are free to eat from any tree in the garden; but you must not eat from the tree of the knowledge of good and evil, for when you eat from it you will certainly die" (Gen. 2:16–17). God's instruction is always in the context of His great blessing. There was no need to eat from the tree. But then Satan showed up.

Satan challenged God's Word: "Did God really say . . . ?" Satan challenged God's trustworthiness: "You will not certainly die." Satan challenged God's motives: "When you eat from [the tree] your eyes will be opened, and you will be like God, knowing good and evil" (Gen. 3:1–5). Eve bought what Satan was selling. She processed his reasoning and decided to trust him instead of God. You can imagine the many thoughts spinning in her mind.

"When the woman saw that the fruit of the tree was good for food and pleasing to the eye, and also desirable for gaining wisdom, she took some and ate it. She also gave some to her husband, who was with her, and he ate it" (Gen. 3:6).

As a result of Eve's and Adam's self-counsel, sin entered the world. As poison at the beginning of a stream contaminates the entire stream, so sin has contaminated us all. Self-counsel leads us to embrace the lies of Satan and ignore the promises of God.

Ignoring God

Although the poison of sin was passed on to the entire stream of humanity, the destruction is vividly demonstrated in Adam and Eve's oldest son. Cain entered into destructive self-counsel after God rejected his offering but accepted his brother's sacrifice. Cain became very angry and the rage showed on his face. God warned Cain, "Sin is crouching at your door; it desires to have you, but you must rule over it" (Gen. 4:7). However, Cain's emotions disregarded God's counsel. In an act of anger he murdered his brother, Abel.

Self-counsel will eventually lead to sin's mastery over our thoughts and actions. God's instruction is pushed aside; His truth is discounted. We give in to our sinful thinking, are absorbed by our sinful desires, and move to sinful action. Self-counsel sidelines God.

Sarah's "Success"

Sarah heard God's promise. God assured a great nation would come through her and Abraham. But time was not on her side. Sarah was well past childbearing years. The long wait for an heir tried her patience. Doubting God's ability to deliver, she took matters into her own hands. Like a father walking his daughter down the aisle, Sarah gave her maidservant, Hagar, to Abraham. And her husband was a willing accomplice. Hagar became pregnant. Sarah became jealous. Tension grew in the home, and the tension continues today between Israel and many of the Arab nations that descended from Hagar's son, Ishmael. Sarah's plan "succeeded" and left a legacy of harsh consequences.

Self-counsel leads us to take action . . . any action. We refuse to wait on God. Sometimes the plan "succeeds," leading us to believe our action was right. But sooner or later the consequences will arrive—and sometimes remain for the rest of our lives.

Soothing the Soul with Disobedience

The story of Jacob and Esau is one of rivalry, jealousy, and deception. After Jacob tricked his father into giving him Esau's blessing, Esau entered into self-counsel. He consoled himself with the thought of killing Jacob. "Esau held a grudge against Jacob . . . [and] said to himself, 'The days of mourning for my father are near; then I will kill my brother Jacob'" (Gen. 27:41).

Self-counsel can make disobedience soothing to the soul. In the midst of adultery, men and women convince themselves that they have never been happier. Pornography serves as a sexual respite. We chew on bitterness like tasty morsels. With God out of the picture and obedience off the table, our hearts and minds move to the dark side. Our sinful nature caresses sin and the perverted pleasure is thoroughly enjoyed . . . for a short time.

It's All about Me

In Luke 12, Jesus told a parable about a wealthy farmer whose field produced a bumper crop. The man, who had been doing well for quite some time, built barns to store his grain. But this particular harvest was so large his storage space was not adequate. The new harvest created a new problem that led the farmer into self-counsel. The man "thought to himself, 'What shall I do? I have no place to store my crops'" (v. 17).

The man's self-counsel became self-centered. Even though he knew that everything he had came from God, he chose to leave God out of the picture. He decided to tear down his barns and build bigger ones in order to store all his grain. He said to himself, "You have plenty of grain laid up for many years. Take life easy; eat, drink and be merry" (Luke 12:19). Sadly, the man didn't realize his time was up. God said to him, "You fool! This very night your life will be demanded from you. Then who will get what you have prepared for yourself?" (Luke 12:20). At the end of the day, self-counsel is self-centered—not God-centered.

David Bowie was mourned by many when he passed away in 2016. Following his death, Bowie's producer, Tony Visconti said, "He always did what he wanted to do. And he wanted to do it his way."[3]

The strange spirituality (and, perhaps, self-counsel) of the Rock and Roll Hall of Famer was highlighted when it came to his constantly evolving thoughts about God. In 1992 he knelt onstage before a television audience of an estimated one billion people and recited the Lord's Prayer. In 1993 he claimed a belief in the unquestionable existence of God.[4] But twelve years later, Bowie said that God's existence "is not a question that can be answered. . . . I'm not quite an atheist and it worries me. There's that little bit that holds on: 'Well, I'm *almost* an atheist. Give me a couple of months . . . I've nearly got it right.'"[5]

When Bowie died on January 10, 2016, he was cremated as stipulated in his will, "in accordance with Buddhist rituals."[6] Early in his career, Bowie admitted, "I felt totally, absolutely alone. And I probably was alone because I pretty much had abandoned God."[7]

Bowie made no claims to be a follower of Jesus. But his constantly changing thoughts about God demonstrate the danger and confusion of self-counsel. As believers we don't have to abandon God, and He won't abandon us. But a time, however brief, of sidelining Him by our self-counsel places us on a dangerous path.

How Self-Counsel Leads Us Toward Wrong Thinking

Then there's King David. His self-counsel moved the man of God away from God. Instead of his heart beating in tune with God's heart, David's heart—much like our hearts—beat with the irregular rhythm of doubt and independence. And David's self-counsel led to three unhealthy conclusions.

Doubt: God's Promise Is Not Valid

David convinced himself that Saul's pursuit would be successful. He said in his heart, "One of these days I will be destroyed by the hand of Saul" (1 Sam. 27:1a). The word *destroy* means to "to sweep" or "snatch away." David was under the constant fear that Saul and his three thousand elite warriors were waiting around the next corner. I imagine that many nights David went to sleep thinking, "Yeah, it may have ended well today, but I bet it won't tomorrow . . . or the next day."

David's heart, like ours, beat with the irregular rhythm of doubt and independence.

David's feelings, however, were in direct contrast to God's word. David had been anointed by Samuel to be the next king of Israel. But after nearly a decade of running, he was finding God's promises harder and harder to believe.

That's exactly where David faltered. He knew what God had promised but doubted that God could deliver. Self-counsel leads to distrust. David concluded that God would not deliver him from the hand of Saul. He decided that his best option was to move into the land of the enemy.

Independence: God's Plan Is Not Working

David determined that Saul would one day destroy him. He concluded, "The best thing I can do is to escape to the land of the Philistines. Then Saul will give up searching for me anywhere in Israel, and I will slip out of his hand" (1 Sam. 27:1b).

When you convince yourself that God's promises aren't true and He is not going to help you, the next step is independence. Self-counsel leads to self-directed actions and leaves God out of the picture. You do what you think is best for you at the moment, even if it means escaping to the land of the enemy. Living in enemy territory seems better than resting in God's promises.

Escape: God's Presence Is Not Enough

Self-counsel concludes that God is not enough. I feel that God has left me alone. Therefore, my inclination is to find a place away from God. There I can get things done on my own. There I can find what I am looking for.

Self-counsel leads us to confirm our action by the results. David was convinced that after he escaped to the land of the Philistines, Saul would give up searching for him. And he was right. "When Saul was told that David had fled to Gath, he no longer searched for him" (1 Sam. 27:4). David's plan worked. Saul gave up the pursuit.

Disobedience does not always bring about immediate consequences. Sometimes the escape to enemy territory provides what seems to be a refreshing reprieve. The long trial subsides. The pressure of obedience is relieved. The writer of Hebrews even concedes that the pleasures of sin are fleeting, or enjoyable for a "short time" (see Heb. 11:25). The word translated "fleeting" (*proskairos*) describes something that is seasonal, temporary. Soon the season is over and the short-lived fun comes to a consequential halt. Scottish novelist George Macdonald said it well: "In whatever man does without God, he must fail miserably—or succeed more miserably." David's escape from Saul landed him in a place of new and dangerous consequences.

How Not to Be Your Own Worst Counselor

Long trials, hope deferred, death of dreams, and the exhausting exercise of waiting can bring each one of us to the point of self-counsel. We are all at risk. How can we minimize the danger of giving in and escaping to the land of the enemy? Here are two practical ways to guard against being our own worst counselor.

A Daily Dose of God's Word

There is no better guard against self-counsel than to read God's Word daily. It sounds too easy, too simplistic until you realize the power of Scripture. The Bible is God's love letter to us. In it God provides everything He wants us to know about Him and about ourselves. Through the pages of Scripture, God personally reveals Himself. He explains who He is, who you are in Him, and how you can know Him in an intimate way. Augustine said, "The Holy Scriptures are letters from home."

In the last letter he wrote, the apostle Paul described the significance of God's Word to a young pastor named Timothy. Paul explained:

> *All Scripture is God-breathed and is useful for teaching, rebuking, correcting and training in righteousness, so that the servant of God may be thoroughly equipped for every good work. (2 Tim. 3:16–17)*

God's Word is God-breathed. Using different authors on different continents at different times in history, God inspired His Word to communicate purposefully and personally to you. Like a GPS, Scripture guides you regarding the road you should travel. It tells you when you've taken the wrong turn. It corrects your route by showing you how to get back on the right path. It provides you with the instruction to stay on the right road. The diagram below will help you get a mental picture of this important truth.[8]

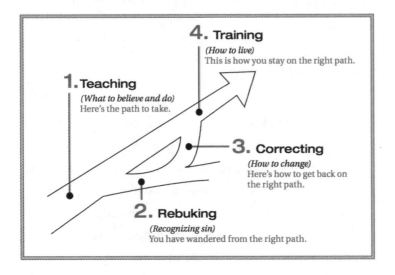

God's Word directs us from our counsel to His (Ps. 73:24). David, on his best days, said that God is the One who counsels him, and when his heart is saturated with Scripture, "even at night my heart instructs me" (Ps. 16:7). Do you ever have nights when you can't go to sleep? You toss and turn and your mind begins to race. Then fear shows up. For those of you going through illness, nights can be the worst time. While others sleep, nights are lonely hours that invite your mind to entertain all the "what ifs," and those "what ifs" never bring comfort. When our eyes are on our challenges, self-counsel takes over. Self-counsel opens the door for fear to walk in unchecked. However, when our focus is on the truth of Scripture, God is the One "who counsels [you]." Even when we are alone, "even at night," comfort and encouragement is delivered to the heart focused on God's Word.

The writer of Hebrews explains that Scripture is living and active. It penetrates our inmost being and judges our thoughts and intentions (Heb. 4:12). Reading God's Word every day protects us from self-counsel. C. H. Spurgeon wrote, "A Bible that's falling apart usually belongs to someone who isn't." You cannot move from self-counsel unless you are absorbing the counsel of God on a regular basis.

A Commitment to Community

The remedy for self-counsel begins with a steady dose of God's Word. It continues when we are committed to doing life with other believers. The Christian life was never meant to be lived solo. David's position of leadership left him in a lonely place. There was no one to check his self-counsel, no one to challenge his decision. Our greatest strength is often our greatest weakness. David's strong gift of leadership left him alone and vulnerable.

In Judges 18, the tribe of Dan was looking for a place of their own where they could settle. They sent five men on a mission to find land that would support their tribe. The five men searched throughout the area and then came to a place called Laish.

There they found a people living in safety, security, and prosperity. But here's the telltale sign. They lived a long way from their neighbors and "had no relationship with anyone else" (Judg. 18:7). The people of Laish thought that they were safe and secure. But they were isolated and alone. They were sitting ducks. The Danites took the city easily because "there was no one to rescue them . . . they lived a long way from Sidon and had no relationships with anyone else" (Judg. 18:28).

Self-counsel led the people of Laish to a false sense of self-confidence. Alone, they were left unsuspecting and vulnerable. Eugene Peterson says it this way:

> *If we stay at home by ourselves and read the Bible, we are going to miss a lot, for our reading will be unconsciously conditioned by our culture, limited by our ignorance, distorted by unnoticed prejudices. In worship we are part of "the large congregation" where all the writers of Scripture address us, where hymn writers use music to express truths which touch us not only in our heads but in our hearts, where the preacher who has just lived through six days of doubt, hurt, faith and blessing with the worshipers, speaks the truth of Scripture in the language of the congregation's present experience. We want to hear what God says and what he says to us: worship is the place where our attention is centered on these personal and decisive words of God.*[9]

Connection in community is essential to protecting ourselves from self-counsel. You need to know someone and someone needs to know you. We need to be surrounded by godly advisers (Prov. 15:22). We need people in our lives who love us enough to tell us that our thoughts and actions are off track even when it hurts. "Wounds from a friend can be trusted" (Prov. 27:6). We need others to encourage and pray for us through the long trials and fatigue of obedience. "As iron sharpens iron, so one person sharpens another" (Prov. 27:17).

When we are struggling we are tempted to isolate ourselves, to run from the very people we need. But remember the worn-out pastor's words from chapter 1, "It's okay to not be okay." We are all fellow strugglers on the journey. We need each other. Self-counsel most often leads us down the path we want to take, unaware of the dangers ahead. But life in community provides the help and encouragement we desperately need.

I remember a time when an elder at our church lost his job. As he searched for a new position he asked the rest of the elders to pray that he would be a witness to God's faithfulness through this difficult time. Instead of isolating himself, he opened up to those around him. Knowing the danger of self-counsel, he desired others to help him keep a proper focus in order to be a godly example. This wise man knew the truth of Proverbs: "Victory is won through many advisers" (11:14).

Another proverb says, "As water reflects the face, so one's life reflects the heart" (27:19). This is what began to happen to David. The long trial had taken its toll. David became his own worst counselor. He convinced himself that the best thing he could do was escape to the land of the Philistines. The man after God's own heart crossed over to live with the enemy and settled in Ziklag.

It was there that David's inner struggle began to show up in his actions. Self-counsel led the man of God into a life of hypocrisy, duplicity, and cover-up . . . as we shall see.

Reflect

1. Look back on some situations in your life when you rationalized actions that were unwise or even harmful. What happened? What did you learn?

2. Check out the chart on page 104. Why is reading God's Word an essential guard against self-counsel?

3. Describe a time when you felt God's plan was not working and you decided to take matters into your own hands.

4. Explain the dangers of being disconnected from community as it relates to self-counsel. Have you been tempted to isolate yourself during hard times?

CHAPTER 6

INTO ENEMY TERRITORY

The man who lies to himself and listens to his own lie
comes to such a pass that he cannot distinguish the truth
within him, or around him, and so loses all respect for
himself and for others.[1]—FYODOR DOSTOYEVSKY,
THE BROTHERS KARAMAZOV

I met Ian, a man in his forties, during his first visit to our church. Ian explained that he had been on staff at a church in another part of the country. He added that it was his first worship service in a long time to be an attendee and not have a role to play in the service. Later, in an email, he shared his story.

Ian had been immersed in ministry for more than two decades. He had served in a variety of positions, most recently as executive pastor. However, Ian explained that he had recently resigned his position because of his double life and the many mistakes and bad choices that came with it. Along with the waves of shame that he had disappointed so many people,

Ian mourned the loss of his once-close relationship with his teenage son. Separated from his wife, Ian felt quite alone in the world. His sadness was all the more poignant because much of his pain was self-inflicted. He wrote, "I keep wishing I could run the tape back on the last ten years."

I don't know where Ian's descent started. Maybe he spent more time teaching about God than desiring to know God. Maybe the constant use of his gifts led him to a weary and vulnerable state. Maybe he became overwhelmed by expectations and looked for an escape. Maybe someone said or did something to hurt him, and he let cynicism and disillusionment drive him off the path. (One friend calls this the "I've known suffering in my life, so I'm always the good guy" mindset, a very subtle trap where we think being hurt lets us off the hook for our bad choices.)

Or maybe sin drove him to isolate himself—something many of us tend to do when we're struggling. I spoke with a teenager recently who had made some costly decisions. Knowing that she had a godly mentor, I asked, "How did you hide this sin from her?" She explained that over time she withdrew from her mentor and isolated herself. Alone, she charted her own path, ignoring wise counsel. Then, like Ian, she packed her bags and moved to Ziklag.

Moving for Good—or Just Visiting?

When I am worn out, I am tempted to give in. Soul weariness attacks my spiritual immune system and dulls my spiritual senses. I don't want to abandon God; I just want to take a break from Him for a while. During these times I can too easily move from what I know to be right and cross over to Ziklag.

Unfortunately, sometimes our Ziklag detour lasts a little longer than a quick break. Soul weariness deludes us into thinking that we can take a short vacation from God. So, as a tourist explores the sights of a city, we take time to check out the alluring attractions. In Ziklag, we fall back into old sinful patterns, ignore the dangers, and embrace the sin. We engage in gossip, because—let's admit it—gossip is fun. The quick clicks to inappropriate sites become planned destinations. The social media message turns into a conversation we should not be having. Most telling, we purposely remain disconnected from God, neglecting prayer and putting our Bible on a shelf. Then one day, we are jolted back to our senses and return to the land of obedience with a holy fear of what an extended stay could have birthed.

I don't want to abandon God; I just want to take a break from Him for a while.

Sometimes our time in Ziklag is neither quick nor short. We choose to relocate—permanently. We convince ourselves that the land of obedience is actually the cause of our discouragement and disappointment. And we set up camp in enemy territory.

Danger Signs

We all have times of struggle, dry times, doubting times, times when maybe our thinking doesn't square with the counsel of God's Word or our behavior is less than admirable. That is the life of faith—ups and downs and everything in between.

o how do we know if we are in danger of landing in Ziklag? What are some of the signs that show we are soul weary and at risk?

1. *"I have lost the desire to read God's Word and pray."* As we have discussed in previous chapters, God's Word is His love letter to us. It tells us who He is, how we can know Him and live for Him. In His Word, God tells His children when we are on the right path, when we have taken a detour, how to get back on the right path, and how to stay on the right path (2 Tim. 3:16–17). Without that divine GPS we are headed to Ziklag.

2. *"I am not moved by experiences that used to give me spiritual goose bumps."* The songs that made me cry now leave my emotions flat. I might as well be singing "Take Me Out to the Ball Game" as "How Great Thou Art." Same goes with hearing how God is at work in a person's life: the story that showed me God's great power now leaves me spiritually numb or inwardly skeptical.

3. *"I get nothing out of church."* Since worship is what I give to God, this statement is a telltale sign. Believers on the road to Ziklag spend more time evaluating than engaging. The songs are too loud or not loud enough, the worship leaders are performing instead of leading, the sermon is too deep or not deep enough, the presentation is never up to par, and the person sitting next to you had the gall not to converse during the meet-and-greet time.

Granted, there are times when the sermon is boring, the music doesn't connect, and the person sitting next to you is a snob—sorry, Christian snob. But here I am talking about falling into the *habit* of negativism—an attitude of criticism that permeates our outlook, a self-absorption that turns all focus inward, an apathy that loses a sense of desire and passion.

This danger sign usually moves a person to check out of church altogether. After all, the reasoning goes, the place is filled with a bunch of hypocrites, a big room of "holier-than-thous." *I just don't need church in my life right now*, we can think.

4 *"I am tired of waiting on God."* God seems silent. I am worn out from praying. I need to take matters into my own hands. It might include cutting some ethical corners; it might include giving in to those nagging sins; it might include taking a hiatus from God ("I'm not even sure He'll know I'm gone"). The best thing I can do is escape to Ziklag.

If you are living in Ziklag as you read these words, you know it. Somewhere along the journey you lost a sense of intimacy with God and became indifferent toward spiritual things. You surrendered to sin—and settled for a life of disobedience, disconnected from God. You no longer fight the temptation; you embrace the sin. It's everyone else's fault, of course. And God is at the top of the list of those who "caused" you to cross over into enemy territory.

I pray that God will use these warning signs to help you realize what is at stake, reconnect with Him, and by His grace move back home.

A Life of Lies

Ziklag is not a place where we relax and recover. It is a place to engage—albeit in the wrong things. During his time in Ziklag, David and his men took day trips to raid three groups of people who were enemies of Israel—the Geshurites, the Girzites, and the Amalekites (1 Sam. 27:8–10).

These raids against the enemies of Israel illustrate an interesting phenomenon about living in Ziklag. For the believer, there remains a desire to please God even when we distance ourselves from Him.

But life in Ziklag demands a life of lies. David had to bend the truth when he gave his activity reports to Achish. When Achish asked David where he had been raiding, David lied. He reported that he had been leading raids against the enemies of the Philistines (1 Sam. 27:10).

In Ziklag, David had to hide his lies, which led him to do the unthinkable. When David raided Israel's enemies he did not leave a man or woman alive, "for he thought, 'They might inform on us and say, "This is what David did."' And such was his practice as long as he lived in Philistine territory" (1 Sam. 27:11).

Lies hidden by murder. David covered up his deceit by burying all those who could tell the truth about his actions. A life of lies and cover-up is a lot of work.

Sin Never Rides Alone

Sin always comes in a "two-for-one" package. Like gangs of outlaws in the Old West, sin never rides alone. When one sin gallops up, you can be sure its partners are galloping alongside. Jealousy rides with envy, gossip, and slander. Pride sits tall in the saddle with selfishness, defensiveness, and greed kicking up dust by its side. Unforgiveness runs with bitterness. Lust takes the back roads with promiscuity, pornography, and adultery. Coveting stays a length in front of stealing. One sin leads to another and leaves a dusty trail of destruction. It's been that way since Adam and Eve.

- In the garden of Eden the first couple had everything they could ever want, everything they would ever need. But the desire to be like God, prodded by Satan's deceit, led to blatant disobedience. As Adam stood passively by, Eve ate the forbidden fruit and handed it to her husband, who took a bite as well. When they realized their sin, they "made coverings for themselves" (Gen. 3:7) and hid from God. And we've been trying to cover up our sin ever since.

- Jealousy led Cain to take his brother Abel "out to the field" to murder him. When God asked Cain, "Where is your brother Abel?" he replied sarcastically, "I don't know. Am I my brother's keeper?" (Gen. 4:9).

- In Genesis 31, Rachel stole household idols from her father and put them inside her camel's saddle. When confronted she lied about her womanly ways to conceal the sin.

- Joseph's brothers were overcome with jealousy and planned to kill him. Instead the brothers sold him into slavery and convinced their father that a wild animal had killed his son (Gen. 37:28–33).

Back to David. Twenty years after his time in Ziklag, and now the king, David had another significant lapse into sin. During a stroll on the roof of his palace, he looked down to see a beautiful woman bathing. Instead of turning away he stopped to stare, filling his heart with lust. David summoned Bathsheba to his palace and a night of passion led to an unplanned pregnancy. After two unsuccessful cover-up attempts, David devised a plan to ensure the death of Bathsheba's husband on the battlefield. David's gang of sin: Coveting, stealing, adultery, lying, and murder (2 Samuel 11). And hurting other people. Which leads us to another danger of soul weariness . . .

Focusing on Ourselves, Forgetting Others

Mitchell was one of the most intelligent and reflective people I have ever met. He loved to ask probing questions that made people think about their legacy. His favorite, usually dropped like a bomb in the midst of lighthearted conversation, was "So, what do you want written on your tombstone?" I remember one person getting that question just as he clamped his teeth around a fully loaded bratwurst at a cook-out. The poor guy almost started choking.

The disappointment and disillusionment that comes with spiritual fatigue turns our hearts inward.

While Mitchell's question isn't on the list of "Top Ten Conversation Starters," you have to admit it's a good one. How we live today determines how we will be remembered tomorrow. We make countless decisions that impact many people in that "dash" between our birthdate and death date. That's why soul weariness and the ensuing stops in Ziklag are so dangerous.

We earlier spoke of the "I'm the good guy" trap many of us fall into. A close cousin is the inward turning that accompanies disappointment and disillusionment. We're hurt and angry; we've been burned, so we tend to focus on ourselves—our feelings and our desires of the moment. Understandable, in a way. But too often our self-counsel leaves others, even those we love, out of our decision-making process. When spiritual fatigue causes me to take matters into my own hands and do what I feel is best, chances are high that many people are going to be impacted . . . and not in a positive way.

When a national championship NCAA football team was put on probation a few years ago, the star player said, "I say 'sorry' to all the fans across the country. I never meant to hurt anybody directly or indirectly with my conduct off the field and I am truly sorry."

Those are the sentiments of many—after the fact. That's what happens in Ziklag. We hurt other people, even though we "never meant to." We seemingly act out of character. Our judgment becomes clouded. This account of David shows the king acting in ways that make us wonder, *David, what were you thinking?*

One day Philistine scouts learned that Israel's army was close by. The five Philistine leaders decided to mount a surprise attack on Saul and his men in Jezreel. The Philistines organized their men into five fighting units numbering hundreds and thousands. David and his men joined Achish and took up their position in the rear. You have to wonder what was going through David's mind—he was preparing to fight his own people! Two times he had the chance to kill Saul; each time he refused. But now David lined up and prepared to do battle with the nation God had promised he would rule. After being worn down from running and living a contradictory life in Ziklag, David wasn't thinking straight.

David and his men were preparing for battle when four of the Philistine leaders challenged Achish about David's motives. Achish trusted David and assured the leaders, "He has already been with me for over a year, and from the day he left Saul until now, I have found no fault in him" (1 Sam. 29:3). However, after a heated debate they couldn't take the risk of David and his men turning against them and joining Israel in the battle.

When Achish delivered the news, David didn't take it well. His emphatic questions reveal his frustration: "But what have I done? What have you found against your servant from the day I came to you until now? Why can't I go and fight against the enemies of my lord the king?" (1 Sam. 29:8.) The decision, however, was final. David and his men left the battle lines and returned to Ziklag.

Did David plan to turn on the Philistines during the battle? Was his desire to fight Israel part of a scheme to destroy the Philistines? Or did the Ziklag life of lies and cover-up dull his reasoning? We will never know for sure, but we do know that life in our personal Ziklag dulls our senses and strips away rational thinking. What other explanation is there for a man to leave his wife and children for a woman who was willing to leave her husband and children? How can a person in an affair ever trust the adulterous partner? Except . . . for the effect of continued sin that dulls our conviction and blinds our spiritual sight.

The Trail of Hurt and Pain

The decisions we make today matter for tomorrow—to us and to those around us. As I write I think of many spiritual leaders whose unfortunate stories are well documented. Stories of hubris that blew up an entire network of churches, addictions that led to bad decisions, and, of course, the all-too-familiar stories of sexual sin. The congregations are left disillusioned and feeling betrayed. One friend became the pastor of a church where the previous pastor had an affair. He told me that his first year was spent more as a grief counselor than a pastor. For twelve months he had to convince the congregation that they could trust him. Another friend followed a leader whose decisions saddled the church with a mountain of debt. He and his congregation spent years digging out of a financial hole. In these cases trust in leadership is damaged and it takes time to build it back . . . for those who stay. Unfortunately, many of those hurt check out of church altogether.

Beyond church leaders, I think of others whose friends and loved ones moved to enemy territory. The people who moved to Ziklag were at one time walking with God—and then they walked away, leaving a trail of hurt and pain. I have counseled wounded individuals who cared enough to confront a friend headed to Ziklag, but ended up estranged from their friend, accused of being judgmental. I have prayed with devastated parents whose children moved into the Ziklag of addictions. I have stood with broken husbands and wives who, through sobs, told me their spouse said, "I don't love you anymore." I have seen children embittered by the desertion, abuse, or abandonment of a parent. I have spoken to employers struggling to come to grips with how their Christian employee had stolen from the company.

We are all at risk. Yes, Ziklag is a foreign country for followers of Christ. We don't belong there. But soul weariness makes the strongest believer vulnerable and makes Ziklag look inviting. Remember Paul's warning to the believers in Corinth: "So, if you think you are standing firm, be careful that you don't fall!" (1 Cor. 10:12.)

And remember: you never go to Ziklag alone. Your trip impacts those you leave behind.

As inviting as Ziklag may seem, life there is not as easy as it looks from the outside.

A Not-So-Relaxing Escape

Ziklag is an attractive escape when we are spiritually exhausted. We go there to take a break from God. But once in Ziklag, we find just how much effort moving away from God really is. We have to wear a concealing mask, convince others that we've never been better, and plan our actions so others don't find out.

Presentation: The Mask

The double life burns energy in the effort to keep up appearances. David's life in Ziklag was characterized by trying to impress Achish, when all along David knew he was living a lie before God, his men, and their families.

Occasionally Lori and I will go to an expensive restaurant for a special evening. Sitting by the window overlooking the beautiful city of Pittsburgh provides an extraordinary ambiance and view. After we are seated, at just the right time, a well-trained waiter brings the menu and gives the well-rehearsed special items of the day. The waiter is normally a Pittsburgher speaking with a French accent. That spectacle alone distracts me from hearing anything about the specials. After he leaves, I take a bite of the hot bread with special butter and look at the menu for myself. It's in English, but I

Once in Ziklag, we find out how much effort moving away from God really is.

can't recognize a word. Everything, even the basic food groups, is presented with a fancy name and unrecognizable description. Then, when whatever I ordered comes, Lori says, "What a beautiful presentation!" I say, "Where's the rest of the food?" Dessert is the same way. A little piece of something with fine lines of chocolate drizzled all around the plate. When I have to lick the plate to get my chocolate fix, there's not enough chocolate!

Presentation is heavy on appearance but light on substance. When you move to Ziklag you resort to impressing people, masking your distance from God. Life in Ziklag demands that you talk and act in ways that make people think you are spiritually full, even though you know that you are running on fumes. You can't keep up the façade.

In the New Testament, Jesus offered forgiveness to the prostitute and salvation to the woman at the well who had made a hobby out of husbands. He had dinner with the self-serving tax collector. He even showed mercy to the thief on the cross. But he had little patience with the Pharisees who were all about presentation. Jesus told them that like whitewashed tombs, they looked "beautiful on the outside but on the inside are full of the bones of the dead." Although they appeared to be righteous, they were like an actor, pretending to be someone they were not (Matt. 23:27–28).

Promotion: "I'm Doing Great!"

Trusting God demands that we wait on His timing and plan. When we become convinced that God is not going to deliver, at least on our timetable, our capacity to trust wears thin and we take matters into our own hands. We reason that since God won't get the job done we need to promote our needs and ourselves.

David's Ziklag experience led him to promote himself in the eyes of Achish. Remember, David lied to Achish about whom he was plundering. The Philistine king thought that David was raiding the people of Israel. "Achish trusted David and said to himself, 'He has become so obnoxious to his people, the Israelites, that he will be my servant for life'" (1 Sam. 27:12).

Life in Ziklag leaves God out of the picture and promotes self. Like a chameleon, we change our colors to fit in or impress a certain group. People caught in the Ziklag of a double life change their language, attitudes, and stories to gain acceptance with the different groups of their network.

A revealing sign that you have settled into the double life of Ziklag is when a work associate, classmate, or parent of a player on the rec team you coach sees you in church and says, "Wow, I didn't expect to see you here!" Recently a friend said of his son's college coach, "He and his wife are believers. At least that's what they say. But during the game he is on the sideline ranting and raving like every other NCAA coach intent on winning." A double life is confusing. It raises the question, "Who are you . . . really?"

Protection

David crossed over into enemy territory to protect himself. Convinced that God would not deliver on his promise and that Saul would kill him, David concluded that it would be better to live with the enemy than to die depending on God.

Ziklag is the place to go when you don't want someone to find out where you are, who you are, or what you are doing. Ziklag is the settlement of a person cutting ethical corners in business or playing games with bank accounts. Ziklag is the destination spot for all who choose to live in sexual sin. Ziklag is the place you go to hide—from God and from those in your life. Ziklag is a city full of those who have succumbed to pornography. You can't have that stuff on your computer with your wife and children around. Ziklag is the place you settle to keep your secrets. Of course, sooner or later, your address is discovered. Sooner or later, you "may be sure that your sin will find you out" (Num. 32:23).[2]

Remember, sometimes we don't move to Ziklag but still demonstrate Ziklag traits. That's what happened to the apostle Peter. When a certain group was present, he was happy to eat with Gentiles, even though it was frowned upon by the Jews of the day. Then, when a group of Jewish believers came to town, Peter changed his colors and "separate[d] himself from the Gentiles because he was afraid" of what the Jews would think. Paul confronted Peter for his duplicity (Gal. 2:11–13).

The Dangers of the Double Life

While I was preaching through the Ziklag series, a retired FBI agent who serves in our church sent me a fascinating email about undercover agents. He explained that when agents are placed in undercover assignments, they are totally separated from friends and family by hundreds of miles and are under regular contact with a specially trained control agent, who is required to closely monitor the undercover agent's physical and psychological safety.

Agents are put undercover with strict limits on the time that they may serve. Unfortunately agents often find themselves in the middle of an assignment when their "time" runs out, and as one supervisor said, "It's kind of hard to pull a UCA out of an assignment because his time is up when he is about to buy some nuclear materials from a group of foreign terrorists."

At the completion of an undercover assignment, agents return to their true identity and are either promoted to head-quarters or offered a transfer to a field office in another area of the country. After a short time to decompress they are often right back in a full investigative workload.

After a number of years in the bureau and having worked in two long-term undercover operations, my friend said he noticed that many agents ran into problems on undercover assignments. In addition to issues with drugs and alcohol, a noticeable number of them have been arrested for shoplifting. He found it inter-esting that an intelligent and highly trained former agent could fool mobsters, KGB agents, and international terrorists, but be unable to escape detection by a Walmart security guard. When my friend asked a behavioral scientist why this was the case, he said, "That is because they want to be caught." The scientist explained that the agents spent a lot of time with some really bad people, and many were conflicted by their duplicitous lives accompanied by unresolved guilt and shame. The constant lies and deceptive lifestyles caused them to adapt in real life to maintain their undercover roles. My friend said, "Even the best of the best have a tough time living a double life."

Sooner or later, the pressures of living undercover catch up with us. The Russian writer Fyodor Dostoyevsky captures the life of Ziklag well in his classic novel *The Brothers Karamazov*. Dostoyevsky wrote:

> *The man who lies to himself and listens to his own lie comes to such a pass that he cannot distinguish the truth within him, or around him, and so loses all respect for himself and for others. And having no respect he ceases to love, and in order to occupy and distract himself without love he gives way to coarse pleasures . . . all from continual lying to other men and to himself.*[3]

Soul weariness makes Ziklag look attractive . . . at least from a distance. But once we move into town we learn that Ziklag is a dangerous place to live. The pressures of living undercover catch up with us. If you are living in Ziklag, it's time to move home.

Regrets and Restoration

Satan wants you to stay in Ziklag. He knows that you are a child of God and will forever be. He also knows that you are rendered ineffective while living in enemy territory. Satan highlights our regrets—the many words we wish could be taken back, the decisions we would like to undo, the actions that brought unwanted and lasting consequences. Satan wants all believers who have settled in Ziklag to believe they have to settle for Ziklag. But, remember, he is a liar and the father of lies.

The Old Testament prophet Joel described a day when a large locust plague and drought would devastate the land of Israel as a consequence of their sin. The army of locusts not only eliminated the growing crops but others to follow. That's like the Ziklag experience. Addictions, bad decisions, divorce, abuse, and many other sins bring a horde of consequences that come in like locusts devastating us and the people in our lives. You wonder if you can ever recover from the days of spiritual ruin in Ziklag. Satan says you can't. But God says you can!

Through the prophet God promised, "I will repay you for the years the locusts have eaten" (Joel 2:25). Speaking as though compelled by legal obligation, God promised to "repay" the nation for the crops the locust had destroyed. God's gracious action prompted the people to praise His name for the wonders He worked among them.[4]

Don't settle for a life in Ziklag. Come home and leave your regrets behind. God graciously desires to bring restoration and redeem the years the locusts devoured. We will consider God's great grace of recovery in the following chapters. But for now, use the following prayer to begin your journey out of Ziklag:

> *Father, I am sorry for my time in Ziklag. I am sorry for my sin against You. I am sorry for the pain my sin has caused others in my life. I desire to turn from my sin and turn to You. I desire to follow hard after You. I have wasted some precious years of my life. Please redeem the time Ziklag robbed. Thank You for Your great grace. I wait on You to do Your work in my life. In Jesus' name. Amen.*

Reflect

1. Ziklag is that place we go in order to take a "break" from God. What are some circumstances that cause you to want to distance yourself from God—at least for a short time?

2. Reflect on a time when you escaped to "enemy territory"— for a quick trip, short stay, or extended visit. What led you to cross over? What characterized your life while visiting or living in Ziklag?

3. What practical steps will you take today to stay away from Ziklag, whether your time there is short or extended?

4. How you live today will determine what you leave tomorrow. What are the things you need to start doing today in order to leave the legacy you desire?

5. We are not meant to walk alone through the Christian life. According to Galatians 6:1-2 we are to carry each other's burdens. One practical application of that instruction is confronting a believer in sin with the purpose of gently restoring that person. Do you know of a person who has moved to Ziklag? What steps will you take to gently confront that person and invite them to God's gracious embrace?

PART 3

RUNNING HOME

LEAVING ZIKLAG

CHAPTER 7

THE GRACE OF CRISIS

No discipline seems pleasant at the time, but painful. Later on, however, it produces a harvest of righteousness and peace for those who have been trained by it.
—HEBREWS 12:11

Now it is time to go home.

And here is a reminder: The God of the universe will not remain in the back seat you have attempted to put Him in while you drive the dangerous roads of Ziklag. He, who sent His Son to die for your sins on the cross, will not let you wallow in selfishness. There will come a time when He jolts you back into reality, often with a crisis of grace.

I moved to Pittsburgh from Texas to become an associate pastor at The Bible Chapel. After two-and-a-half years the senior pastor left, and I was asked to take his spot. I learned early on that I had a great gift for growing a church. We grew from five hundred to three hundred . . . overnight! The numbers were changing dramatically, but in the wrong direction.

The transition was rocky, to say the least. One group of fifty people left to start a new church less than a mile down the road, while another group told me that they would stick around for six months to "see how things go." Part of seeing "how things go" was evaluating my sermons. Every weekend I felt the pressure of trying to hold on to the people we did have by preaching a sermon that was true to the text, deeply theological, peppered with just the right amount of humor, contained moving illustrations, and included rubber-meets-the-road applications. One man I really wanted to stay gave me a library full of books by Puritan pastors. So of course, I tried to mix in a quote or two that I thought would make him happy.

While the only other pastor on staff was doing a great job in his areas of ministry, I filled my days with operational responsibilities and personal meetings, trying to talk people into remaining at our church. Most of my evenings were tied up teaching a class, meeting with the ministry teams that I had led as an associate, leading elder meetings, editing our monthly newsletter, doing home visitation with new attenders, or dealing with the inevitable life issues of believers in community. On top of everything else we had outgrown our first building and were meeting in a high school and in the process of building a new facility. So, of course, I was a part of the building team.

"Let go of your death grip on My church and trust others to do their part."

We had just moved into a new home, and a swing set stood on the side of our yard. One evening as I was on my way to yet another meeting, I vividly remember pulling out of the driveway and turning onto the street to see Lori and our kids playing on the swing, enjoying the summer evening. Later, Lori said she felt sad seeing me driving away and missing so much time with our children.

Everything I was doing was good stuff, kingdom stuff. But I was exhausting myself spiritually, emotionally, and physically. I was convinced (I am ashamed to say) that I was single-handedly holding the church together. Lori's gentle reminders that I was spending too much time away from home and our children were angrily rebuffed. I murmured in my heart, "Doesn't she realize that I have to do this for God and for my continued employment?"

For several months I took up residence in the Ziklag of self-importance. "The existence of The Bible Chapel depends on me." "People staying at the church depends on me." "Why am I the only one doing all the work?" "Why doesn't anyone else care about the church as much as I do?" I felt alone, but imbued with a sense of pride and hubris. *I* was keeping the church together! I was proud of me . . . but God wasn't.

One day I was planning for an evening meeting. I don't recall what the meeting was about, but one by one those who were supposed to attend called to say they couldn't come, forcing me to cancel the meeting. I was ticked! It played right into my Ziklag mindset that I was the only one who really cared about the church. I remember easing my car into the garage, still angry that the meeting had been canceled. But when I got out of my car, God stopped me before I entered our house. I have never heard God's audible voice, but His message to me was clear. God's gracious confrontation went something like this:

"You fool," I heard Him say, "the most important 'church' you lead is on the other side of that door, and you have been neglecting Lori and your children! You are not holding The Bible Chapel together, I am. Cut your pompous attitude. Let go of your death grip on My church and trust others to do their part. I am God and you are not!"

I felt like I had been awakened from a spiritual stupor. And so, I began my move out of Ziklag. God used one more meeting to drive home His message.

One evening I attended a building team meeting. This group was an all-star team, comprising leaders in some of the top companies in Pittsburgh. But again, I was convinced they couldn't build our church without me. About fifteen minutes into the meeting, one member of the group looked at me and said, "Go home. You don't know a thing about building a building. You need to be with your family. We can handle this without you. Get out of here." God graciously kicked me out of the meeting, and I still thank Him for that firm push out of my Ziklag.

Since that time our church has had four major building efforts plus numerous upgrades to our multisite campuses, and I have not attended building team meetings unless specifically invited. And . . . they have done just fine without me!

I wish I could say that was the last time God had to confront my Ziklag tendencies, but . . . no. I have learned, sometimes the hard way, that God will allow His children to run away—but not for long. In His timing and in His way He jolts us back into reality, often with a gracious intervention. That's what we see in the life of David.

Up in Smoke

Settling in Ziklag always comes at a cost. For more than a year the man after God's own heart put God on the back burner of his heart. David didn't hate God; he just forgot Him. The days turned into weeks and the weeks turned into months. Life moved on until the crisis—the day he and his men returned home to find Ziklag destroyed by the Amalekites, their homes reduced to piles of smoking embers and their families captured.

The emotion of the crisis was unbearable. David and his men "wept aloud until they had no strength left to weep" (1 Sam. 30:4). Close your eyes and imagine these calloused soldiers on their knees, wailing in grief. However, when they had no strength left to weep, remorse turned to resentment. Each man was "bitter in spirit" and turned against David. Settling in Ziklag was David's idea; the raids against the Amalekites had been David's call; and not leaving men in Ziklag to protect the city and their families was David's decision. The waves of sorrow and anger sparked a desire for revenge so strong that the men debated whether or not they should stone David (1 Sam. 30:6).

The Gift of Crisis

When you become a child of God, you will always be His child. Nothing can separate you from God's love "that is in Christ Jesus our Lord" (Rom. 8:38–39). When you run to Ziklag, God will, in His way and timing, get your attention. He will not remain forgotten. He may use a crisis as His gracious way of bringing you back home.

As I write this, I think of many men and women whom I have met with when their sin came to light. They had moved to Ziklag and lived a life of lies and cover-up. It's hard work to manage a secret sin. But at some point, God says, "Enough!"

The affair is exposed. The person you were living with decides to move out. Accounting calls you in to talk about some confusing figures on your expense report. The professor learns you have been cheating on the exams. Your husband sees the messages on Facebook. Your wife sees the texts. An IT person discovers the history of your visits to porn sites. The doctor finally refuses to write another script for the pain pills. Although it may not feel like it at the time, the crisis is an act of God's great grace.

For David, God's gift of crisis was painful. He stood alone grieving the loss of his own family and feeling the weight of letting down his men. He knew that they were seriously discussing dragging him to a rocky area and stoning him. At the moment David's circumstances didn't seem much like a gift. But God used a crisis to turn David's heart back home. He does the same for us.

Crisis can come in a variety of ways, but one phrase sums it up: the Lord's discipline. God loves His children too much to allow them to live at a dangerous distance. He will get our attention, with loving discipline. The writer of Hebrews says,

> *Endure hardship as discipline; God is treating you as his children. For what children are not disciplined by their father? If you are not disciplined—and everyone undergoes discipline—then you are not legitimate, not true sons and*

daughters at all. . . . No discipline seems pleasant at the time, but painful. Later on, however, it produces a harvest of righteousness and peace for those who have been trained by it. (Heb. 12:7–8, 11)

God loves you too much to allow you to stay in Ziklag. Living away from Him is a dangerous and vulnerable place. The life of lies and cover-up impacts you and others. Sometimes you have to hit rock bottom before coming to your senses. Like He did with David, God will bring you to a point of crisis. He started a good work in you and has promised to carry it to completion (Phil. 1:6). God will not let you forget Him. He will not leave you to wallow in the filth of your sin.

God will not let you forget Him.

I don't know how God will get your attention. For some, it is the possibility of losing your family. For others, it is a conviction from the Holy Spirit as they read the Bible. For me it happened in my own garage. God uses different ways to confront us and help us discover that . . .

> . . . our sin has left us alone.
>
> . . . our independence is showing us just how weak we really are.
>
> . . . our supposed freedom was a confining prison.
>
> . . . we have hurt the people we love the most.
>
> . . . forbidden pleasure is followed by mornings of nauseating guilt.
>
> . . . what was so attractive has become so very ugly.

However God gets your attention, I do know that He is waiting for you to leave Ziklag and return home.

The Gracious Father

Jesus once told the story of a young man who moved to his personal Ziklag. The man went to his father and boldly demanded his share of the estate. Normally an estate was not divided among the children until a father was too old to manage the daily operation or had passed away. So, in effect, the son said to his father, "I wish you were dead. I can't wait until you die. I want my money now!" The father obliged.

The son took the money and set off for a distant country—his own personal Ziklag. Money is a magnet for "friends," and they stayed as long as the money was flowing. The son was immersed in wine, women, and song . . . heavy on the women. But it wasn't long before he had squandered all his inheritance on what Jesus described as "wild living." The "friends" deserted him, the women couldn't be bought, and "he began to be in need." Penniless and alone, he took the only job he could find—feeding pigs. He was so hungry that the food he was feeding the animals looked appetizing. Knee-deep in pig slop, the young man came to a point of crisis and began his journey back home.

Jesus explained the man's awakening as coming "to his senses." That's often how God graciously uses a crisis in our lives. The calamity shakes us awake from a sinful stupor. Our eyes are opened to see that we are knee-deep in sin. And the best part of the gracious awakening is that we realize, "I don't have to stay here!"

The story that Jesus told is often called the Prodigal Son, but I think it is better described as the Gracious Father. The father had been waiting for the day of his son's return. He had longingly looked down the road that led home. And then, one day, he saw the shadowy figure of his son and "while he was still a long way off, his father saw him and was filled with compassion for him; he ran to his son, threw his arms around him and kissed him" (Luke 15:20). The son started to give his heartfelt confession, "I am no longer worthy to be called your son; make me like one of your hired servants" but the father wouldn't hear of it. He said, "'Quick! Bring the best robe and put it on him. Put a ring on his finger and sandals on his feet. Bring the fattened calf and kill it. Let's have a feast and celebrate. For this son of mine was dead and is alive again; he was lost and is found.' So they began to celebrate" (Luke 15:22–24).

The Gracious Crisis

God graciously confronted David with a crisis. Ziklag was burned to the ground and all the families of his soldiers had been taken captive. The damage was almost deadly as David's men contemplated killing him. God brought David to the point where his only option was God. Alone and broken, David found that when God is all you have, God is all you need.

This truth is not only learned in times of rebellion. Uninvited and unexpected storms hit and leave us reeling. But even in our questions the truth of God's sufficiency can be experienced.

Standing by the freshly dug grave, I watched a heavy-hearted couple make their way up a steep hill. The father served as the lone pallbearer. Only one was needed to carry the casket holding the body of his infant son. He placed it on the nylon straps that would lower the small casket into the grave. What do you say to a couple that has lost a child? I remember only hugs and tears as we waited for the rest of the family to gather on the windy hillside.

I said a few words that seemed so inadequate. A relative spoke as well, and I was thankful for his personal and comforting remarks. Then the father spoke. His words were emotional but strong, and right from Scripture. Over the sound of the wind blowing through the nearby trees, he said, "The LORD gave and the LORD has taken away; may the name of the LORD be praised" (Job 1:21b).

Here in this statement, first uttered by Job after his tragic loss, are words declaring the sovereignty of God and man's only proper response. With broken hearts, tearful eyes, and quivering lips, we acknowledge that God is the giver of our first breath and the One who determines our last. Even through our pain we declare His praise.

God's grace of crisis leads us to the bedrock truth of our life: when God is all you have, God is all you need.

I don't know where you are as you read this chapter. Maybe your rebellious life has led you to settle in Ziklag. Or maybe disappointment or discouragement caused you to slowly slip away. You know you are in Ziklag but don't remember actually moving there. You haven't abandoned God; you have just forgotten Him, for now. Whatever caused the move to Ziklag, I am praying that, like the prodigal son, you come to your senses. I am praying that you will leave the distant country and head back home. I can promise that the Father is waiting. His arms are wide open. He is ready to forgive and restore. But *you* have to respond to God's gracious confrontation and make the journey back home. It's time, isn't it? It's time! And remember—when God is all you have, God is all you need. God and the strength He provides are all you will ever need.

Reflect

1. What caused the prodigal son to move to his personal Ziklag? Have you ever had these same desires? How did you respond?

2. Dietrich Bonhoeffer explains that there are times in our lives when God "is quite unreal to us. . . . Satan does not fill us with hatred of God, but with forgetfulness of God."[1] Describe a time when God became unreal to you.

3. Describe a time when God used a crisis to get your attention.

4. In Jesus' story, the prodigal son came to his senses and returned home. Reflect on the way Jesus describes the gracious father.

5. Ziklag is not a place to abandon God; it's the place we go to forget Him. But the almighty God will not be forgotten. How does God remind you of His presence and love in your life?

CHAPTER 8

THE GRACE OF STRENGTH

Surely the awesome Spirit of God wishes to do more within us than what is presently going on! There are scars He wants to heal. There are insights He longs to reveal. There are profound dimensions of life He would dearly love to open up.[1] —CHARLES SWINDOLL

The meeting took place more than twenty years ago, and it still haunts me. A young couple had been attending our church and wanted to get married. From our conversations they were very new in the faith, but it was evident that God was at work in their hearts. We had some great interaction. However, as we started talking about the process of premarital counseling I learned some disconcerting news.

The couple was living together. Since living together before marriage is contrary to God's plan (and 70 percent of those who live together before marriage never make it to their tenth anniversary), I explained that I couldn't officiate their wedding unless they made separate living arrangements during their engagement. After several minutes of discussion and reasoning, the young woman got up and ran out of my office. The confused man looked at me and said, "What do I do now?" I asked that he let her know how much we cared for them and why we desired for them to live apart until marriage. We prayed. He left. And I never saw either of them again.

What still haunts me is that I was asking them to leave Ziklag on their own strength, and at that point in their lives they couldn't do it on their own. I don't know if the situation would have ended differently had I said any more. I just wish my encouragement had focused on God's strength to enable them to do what He was calling them to do.

As I write this I can feel the anguish of many others I've met with over the years trying to make a decision about their stay in Ziklag. The internal struggle is palpable. Some feel caught in sin, like a fish with a hook deep in its throat. They feel unable to leave, too far in to get out. For sure, sometimes it's an excuse to continue in sin's season of pleasure. Other times shame and guilt paralyzes the soul.

Other people who have sat across from me are fearful of what will happen if they do leave. Will his wife take him back? Will the boss let her keep her job? Will their parents let them back in the house? Will leaving Ziklag make them a person without a country? I can still see the pain on one woman's face as she doubted that her husband and children would ever forgive her and invite her back into their lives. She reasoned that living in enemy territory was better than living alone.

Ziklag is an appealing place. Were it not, we wouldn't have moved there in the first place. We can move into Ziklag in our own strength, but it takes much more than willpower to cross the border and head for home. Just ask King David.

Ziklag is an appealing place. Were it not, we wouldn't have moved there in the first place.

When David Stood Alone

David was "greatly distressed." He was deeply grieving the capture of his family and fearing his men, who had now turned on him. The Hebrew word for "distress" means to bind, tie up, to be restricted. After sixteen months David's world was closing in on him. The leader stood alone.

Standing alone is a frightening place to be, isn't it? However, it is always the destination when we choose to move to Ziklag. Sometimes our sin leaves us physically alone: everyone we love leaves. Sometimes our life in Ziklag leaves us emotionally alone. Even when people surround us we feel an inner emptiness. But life in Ziklag always leaves us spiritually distanced. You feel like God is a million miles away, and even if you could find your way back, you are not sure if He wants you. But He does!

In his aloneness and fear and guilt, David had only one place to turn:

> But David found strength in the LORD his God.
> (1 Sam. 30:6b)

What a vivid picture of grace! God had chosen David and empowered him. But David, worn out from running, decided that God either wouldn't or couldn't protect him from Saul. He concluded, "One of these days I will be destroyed by the hand of Saul. The best thing I can do is to escape to the land of the Philistines" (1 Sam. 27:1). As we have seen, during his sojourn in Ziklag David ignored or avoided God. But now, alone and afraid, David turned to God and found strength.

Notice that God did not say, *David, so nice to see you! Where have you been for the last sixteen months?*

God's grace came with unconditional love.

So David, do you think you can ignore Me for a year and just show up and expect My help?

God's grace came tenderly, with no rebuke.

Well, David, I'd love to help you, but you are going to have to work your way back and prove yourself.

God's grace came with no call for penance.

David, you and I both know that you blew it. Big time! Sorry, but you are on your own.

God's grace came with unqualified acceptance.

David turned to God and received the warm embrace of grace. He said, "My soul is weary with sorrow; strengthen me according to your word" (Ps. 119:28). If you are "weary with sorrow," you can learn from David . . .

The Futility of Relying on Ourselves

Depending on our human strength is a failing proposition. When David was worn out by obedience, he counseled himself to move to Ziklag, where the sad saga began. There, in enemy territory, he depended on himself and his military strategy (along with the lies and cover-ups) to keep him in good standing with the Philistine kings. Remember, Ziklag is the place we go to forget God so, with God out of our minds, we have to trust in ourselves—our skills, hard work, relationships.

Seth was a self-made man—or so he thought. With a successful business and growing bank account, he was a regular at our church, involved in significant ministry. Then it all came crashing down. In a period of economic downturn he lost his business and what he believed to be his security. Seth decided to move to Ziklag.

After two years of being AWOL, Seth showed up at a church function. He shared his story with me and said, "When I lost it all I was embarrassed to come to church. I felt like a failure."

I am saddened by how many Christians place their hope in the government and in the platform of governing officials.

It's too easy for each of us to believe our strength comes from the stuff we have. Moses wrote, "You may say to yourself, 'My power and the strength of my hands have produced this wealth for me.' But remember the LORD your God, for it is he who gives you the ability to produce wealth" (Deut. 8:17–18).

Every election season I know the anonymous notes are going to come. I believe every Christian should vote in an informed and prayerful manner. I often distribute a booklet I wrote called *Picking a President* that helps voters look for certain virtues and character traits. But I believe the decision remains between you and God when you cast your ballot. Some disagree (mostly anonymously). They are convinced that

I should promote a certain candidate. I am saddened by how many Christians place their hope in the government and in the platform of governing officials. I often quote Charles Colson (much to the dismay of those who write the anonymous notes), who said that he was confident that "the Kingdom of God would not arrive on Air Force One." Colson's words echo the psalmist:

> No king is saved by the size of his army; no warrior escapes by his great strength. A horse is a vain hope for deliverance; despite all its great strength it cannot save. But the eyes of the LORD are on those who fear him, on those whose hope is in his unfailing love, to deliver them from death and keep them alive in famine. We wait in hope for the LORD; he is our help and our shield. In him our hearts rejoice, for we trust in his holy name. (Ps. 33:16–21)

Most people want to elect strong individuals who will protect our country. This is right and noble, but in Ziklag we will soon discover the futility of depending on our strength. Our strength is found when we turn to God. He is our help and our shield.

Our Weakness, His Strength

Some downplay a person's turning to God as a last option. They roll their eyes when bad health causes us to find strength in God after we have been away from Him. They are suspect of the prodigal son who comes home only after losing everything.

But God never turns us away . . . even when we turn to Him as our last resort. Such is the manner of grace.

Psalm 102 is the cry of a person in pain. The ascription explains that this psalm is "a prayer of an afflicted person who has grown weak and pours out a lament before the LORD." The afflicted said that his "heart is blighted and withered like grass. . . . I groan aloud and am reduced to skin and bones" (vv. 4–5). But even when God was his last resort he was confident that God would "respond to the prayer of the destitute; he will not despise their plea" (v. 17).

Robert is a friend of mine who ran from God for the first forty-six years of his life. Although he was raised in a Christian home, he never trusted in Christ as his personal Savior. In fact, in Robert's words, "I hated Christians." His life became self-absorbed. Success. Position. Money, and all the things money could buy. Then one day while sailing in the Pacific Ocean, he and his crew ran into a terrible storm. That night Robert was certain that he would die. As a last resort, he cried out to God, and in the middle of a raging ocean, God heard his plea.

Robert has been following hard after Jesus for the last twenty years. Today he leads an international ministry focused on teaching God's Word and helping believers grow in their walk with Christ. God hears the prayer of the destitute. He will not "despise their plea."

The fact of the matter is that regardless of the crisis that drives us back to God, we are helpless and hopeless on our best days. In Hebrews 11 the writer lists those who conquered kingdoms, shut the mouths of lions, withstood the flames, and escaped the sword. He describes these faithful men and women as those "whose weakness was turned to strength" (v. 34).

In his book *Mere Apologetics,* Alister McGrath notes that "one of the most familiar criticisms of Christianity is that it offers consolation to life's losers."[2] He goes on to say, "If you have a broken leg, you *need* a crutch. If you're ill, you *need* medicine. That's just the way things are. The Christian understanding of human nature is that we are damaged, wounded, and disabled by sin. That's just the way things are."[3]

In fact, it is our weakness that demonstrates God's strength. In Paul's second letter to the church in Corinth he shared that he had been given a particular affliction. Paul said that he pleaded with God on three separate occasions to take it away. But God said, "My grace is sufficient for you [My lovingkindness and My mercy are more than enough—always available—regardless of the situation] for [My] power is being perfected [and is completed and shows itself most effectively] in [your] weakness" (2 Cor. 12:9 AMP). Strength coming from weakness may seem contradictory, but as one writer says, "Paradoxically, our waving the white flag of submission to God's right over our lives is the key that unlocks the gate to many future victories in his name."[4]

Our Desperate Need for God's Strength

Joshua followed Moses as the leader of the nation of Israel. I cannot think of a more daunting assignment. After all, no one had "ever shown the mighty power or performed the awesome deeds that Moses did in the sight of all Israel" (Deut. 34:12). After Moses died the leadership responsibility fell on Joshua, and it fell hard. God commissioned the fearful leader with words of encouraging exhortation, "Be strong and courageous. . . . Be strong and very courageous. . . . Have I not commanded you? Be strong and courageous. Do not be afraid; do not be discouraged, for the LORD your God will be with you wherever you go" (Josh. 1:6–9).

Joshua had to depend on God at every stage of Israel's journey. In miraculous power the Lord dammed up the Jordan River. As the people crossed over into the Promised Land they looked up to see Jericho—the most fortified city of the world. At every turn there was fear and a call for fresh faith. And at every turn God delivered on His promise. God caused the walls of Jericho to come tumbling down. He will cause whatever is standing between you and a life of faithful obedience to come tumbling down as well.

As uncomfortable as it is for a believer to stay in Ziklag, it is often just as fearful to leave. But God's presence will provide all the strength you need to leave Ziklag. "So do not fear," Isaiah said, "for I am with you; do not be dismayed, for I am your God. I will strengthen you and help you; I will uphold you with my righteous right hand" (Isa. 41:10).

Strength in the Holy Spirit

Just as impossible as it is for us to stay out of Ziklag on our own strength, so it is impossible to leave in our own strength. Thankfully, strength is not self-generated. Believers have the Holy Spirit of the living God residing in them. You can't leave Ziklag on your own—but only by the power of the Holy Spirit.

In his book *Flying Closer to the Flame*, Charles Swindoll explains how believers settle for less than what God has for them through His Spirit. He writes,

> *The inescapable fact is this: Most (yes, most) Christians you and I know have very little dynamic and joy in their lives. Just ask them. They long for depth, for passion, for a satisfying peace and stability instead of a superficial relationship with God made up of words without feelings and struggles without healings. Surely there is more to the life of faith than church meetings, Bible study, religious jargon, and periodic prayers. Surely the awesome Spirit of God wishes to do more within us than what is presently going on! There are scars He wants to heal. There are insights He longs to reveal. There are profound dimensions of life He would dearly love to open up. But not one of the above will happen automatically—not as long as He remains a sterile, untouchable blip on our theological PC. He is the comforting Helper, remember? He is the Truth-Teacher, the will of the Father revealer, the Gift Giver, the Hurt Healer. He is the inextinguishable flame of God, my friend. HE IS GOD. To remain a distance from Him is worse than wrong; it is downright tragic. Flying closer to the flame, therefore, is better than good; it is absolutely magnificent.*[5]

It takes much more than willpower to leave Ziklag and return home. We need the strength of the Holy Spirit. He is the "inextinguishable flame of God." Only He will lead you out of the land of the enemy and back to the land of obedience. And the Father will rejoice in your return!

When we were dating, Lori bought a passage of Scripture written on a parchment-like paper. Together we built a frame for the verse and after we were married it hung in our home for many years. The verse is one of my favorites. When I send a written card of encouragement to someone in our congregation I often write the verse's location, Zephaniah 3:17, under my name. This passage reminds us of five characteristics of the great God who longs for us to come back home and gives us the strength to return.

> *The* LORD *your God is in your midst, a mighty one who will save; he will rejoice over you with gladness; he will quiet you by his love; he will exult over you with loud singing.* (Zeph. 3:17 ESV)

The LORD *your God is in your midst.* The eternal God is always with us. In your great joy or deep sorrow, He is there. He provides comfort, encouragement, instruction, correction, and strength. He will never leave nor forsake you.

A mighty one who will save. Nothing in our lives is too big for God. He will give us all we need to do everything He calls us to do. Rescue from Ziklag is no problem for Him. He is ready to bring you home.

He will rejoice over you with gladness. God sent Jesus to die just for you! That's how much He loves you! You are a child of the living God. He takes great pleasure in you. He rejoices over you with gladness like a loving mom and dad rejoice over their children. You have been away too long. He provides the way back home.

He will quiet you by His love. Life in Ziklag is chaotic. It cranks up the anxiety level, causing stress and doubt. But that's when the Holy Spirit takes over. He breathes calm into our soul. He reminds us that He is on our side.

He will exult over you with loud singing. We know what it's like to sing songs to God. But God tells us that He sings over you! With loud singing! But those songs are hard to hear in Ziklag. By God's strength, come home and hear the Father singing songs of joy just for you!

Whether your Ziklag experience is a quick stop, short visit, or settling down, God has so much more for you than living in enemy territory. The strength to leave Ziklag comes from God alone. The desires to stay away must come from Him as well. God is ready to rescue you from Ziklag!

Reflect

1. Knowing the dangers of Ziklag, why do many Christians choose to stay there?

2. Describe a time in your life when God was all you had. Did you find that He was all you needed? How did this manifest itself?

3. Many believers place their hope in government rather than God. Why are we so tempted to trust in the strength of man rather than the power of God?

4. Describe a time when you faced a daunting assignment and experienced an extraordinary sense of God's strength.

5. Can you relate to, in Charles Swindoll's words, "a superficial relationship with God made up of words without feelings and struggles without healings"? What steps can you take to experience the power of the Holy Spirit in your life?

CHAPTER 9

THE GRACE OF RECOVERY

I exult in the thought that thy justice is satisfied, thy truth established, thy law magnified, and a foundation is laid for my hope. I look to a present and personal interest in Christ and say, Surely he has borne my griefs, carried my sorrows, won my peace, healed my soul.[1] —THE VALLEY OF VISION

Olivia is a young millennial from a strong Christian family. She trusted Christ early in life and grew as a follower of Jesus during her teenage years. Now, having completed college and graduate school, she is back in the Pittsburgh area and attending our church. After I preached a sermon on David's time in Ziklag, Olivia sent me the following note:

> *I can look back to nearly three years ago and watch myself slowly packing my things, slowly beginning the journey to Ziklag and quite easily settling in there. The description of Ziklag, the person it makes you, and the way it affects*

*your life . . . hit me like a ton of bricks. The scariest part
to me was how long I lived there without even realizing or
caring.*

*I began my attempts to move out of Ziklag eight months
ago. Eight months ago! I failed several times, leaving, then
going right back. But in God's incomprehensible forgiveness, patience and mercy, He hung on to me and gave me
the people and tools I needed to leave for good. I can't quite
express the overwhelming relief I feel today to be loved by
such a gracious God that has forgiven me and accepted me
with open arms.*

Olivia made the journey back home. It didn't happen overnight; there were times when she left and then went right back
again. But along the way she encountered God's great strength,
patience, forgiveness, and mercy. Olivia experienced God's
great grace of recovery.

Whether you, like Olivia, journeyed all the way to Ziklag
or were just considering a quick trip there, you can experience
the grace of recovery—relationships mended, "soul weariness"
healed, love for God and the things of God rekindled. It begins
with turning back to God.

David: The Road Back

Remember how the whole Ziklag journey started? Worn out
from running, "David thought to himself, 'One of these days I
will be destroyed by the hand of Saul. The best thing I can do
is to escape to the land of the Philistines. Then Saul will give
up searching for me anywhere in Israel, and I will slip out of

his hand'" (1 Sam. 27:1). Personal pronouns are always dead giveaways. The "I's" and "me's" in this passage provide the evidence that David's fatigue had turned him from trusting God to trusting himself. He determined that God's promise to be Israel's next king would never be fulfilled. David took matters into his own hands and moved to Ziklag. There, the man after God's own heart was forced to live a life of lies and cover-up. Knee-deep in his backfired plan, David's men, who had protected him with their lives, were ready to pelt him with rocks. David stood alone. In that moment of crisis, David turned to God and found, not only strength to stand, but also courage to engage in the gift of recovery.

God, I'm Listening . . . Again

When there was no other place to turn, David turned to God. He asked Abiathar, the priest, to bring the ephod, an ornate vest worn only by the priest and used to discern God's guidance.

David asked the Lord for his next steps: "Shall I pursue this raiding party? Will I overtake them?" David's self-counsel had led him into a desperate situation; now he was determined to follow God and His timing. David's strength and confidence were found in God's answer, "Pursue them. . . . You will certainly overtake them and succeed in the rescue" (1 Sam. 30:8). David did not strike out on his own to pursue Ziklag's attacker. He turned humbly to God—and so must we. Certainly, we don't call on a priest to bring an ephod today. Our guidance and strength is found in Scripture, God's love letter to us.

The Grace of Recovery: Repentance

Here is a special word for those who have truly strayed from God, hurt others, and yet feel a tug back toward Him. Turning back to God also means turning around—that is, repentance. To repent means "to turn back," "return," "to change one's mind or purpose." When we repent, we express contrition, sorrow, for the time away from God. Again, David shows us the way.

Years after living in the actual city, David had another Ziklag experience. He committed adultery with Bathsheba, arranged for her husband's murder, and lived in denial until God confronted him through the prophet Nathan. David's prayer, recorded in Psalm 51, provides the five steps of true repentance.

- **True repentance is a plea for mercy based on God's unchanging character:** "Have mercy on me, O God, according to your unfailing love; according to your great compassion blot out my transgressions" (Ps. 51:1).

David's prayer focuses on two unchanging characteristics of God. The Hebrew word *chesed* describes the unfailing love that God has for His children. The word *racham* describes the great compassion that a mother has for her child. True repentance begins as we cling to God's love and compassion.

- **True repentance acknowledges that all sin is ultimately against God.** "For I know my transgressions, and my sin is always before me. Against you, you only, have I sinned . . ." (vv. 3–4a.)

David's sin had a ripple effect—Bathsheba was compromised, her husband Uriah was killed in battle, the baby born to Bathsheba died. But . . . David realized that, first and foremost, his sin was against God. Our sin hurts others, but the full weight of our wrongdoing is ultimately against God. When we understand and accept that truth, our sin carries the gravity it deserves.

• **True repentance accepts sin's consequences—whatever they are.** "Against you, you only, have I sinned and done what is evil in your sight; so you are right in your verdict and justified when you judge" (v. 4).

God forgives and restores; yet there are costs to our sins, even forgiven sins (Gal. 6:7). We must own our sin *and* its consequences. This is critical for the grace of recovery. A person who is truly repentant is willing to accept the outcomes and say, "God, You are right in your verdict and justified when You judge." Here's how this step of repentance was demonstrated in David's life.

God sent the prophet Nathan to tell David that his sin would be forgiven but his son born to Bathsheba would die. When the newborn became ill, David began a period of fasting and pleaded with God to spare the child. When the boy died a week later, David's advisers were afraid to tell him the news. Since David had been so distraught during the child's illness they feared he might harm himself if he learned the boy had died. But when he got the news he got up, washed, worshiped, and returned home to eat. His servants were puzzled. Why did David fast when the child was alive and feast when the child died? David explained, "While the child was still alive, I fasted and wept. I thought, 'Who knows? The LORD may be gracious to me and let the child live.' But now that he is dead, why should I go on fasting? Can I bring him back again? I will go to him, but he will not return to me" (2 Sam. 12:21–23).

This was not the action of a calloused heart. David experienced grief, like every father who loses a child. But he honored God by accepting the painful outcome of his sin. He declared by his actions that God's verdict was right and his judgment was justified.

I realize that this is a very difficult step of repentance. First, I want to be clear that not every challenge in life is a direct result of sin. In a fallen and sinful world God uses every circumstance to mold you into the person He desires you to be. However, some consequences are directly related to our actions. In these instances many believers will cry, "Foul!" "God's judgment is too hard!" "I can't believe I got fired!" "It's been a week since I confessed my sin and my wife still won't let me back in the house!" "So I lied to my friend, but now she needs to forgive me and move on. Where's the grace?" The grace of recovery begins with repentance, and true repentance accepts the consequences of sin.

- **True repentance desires the resolve to obey.**

> *Cleanse me with hyssop, and I will be clean; wash me, and I will be whiter than snow. Let me hear joy and gladness; let the bones you have crushed rejoice. Hide your face from my sins and blot out all my iniquity. Create in me a pure heart, O God, and renew a steadfast spirit within me. (Ps. 51:7–10)*

The word *create* expresses the idea of "re-forming"; renew means to repair. David prayed that God would reform and repair him, that God would grant him a "willing spirit" that would keep him away from a Ziklag experience (Ps. 51:12).

• **True repentance understands that God desires more than lip service.** In 2 Corinthians 7:10, Paul explains the difference between a worldly sorrow and a godly sorrow. Worldly sorrow is characterized by the feeling, "I am sorry I got caught. Actually the sin was enjoyable. I just wish I hadn't been found out." A person experiencing worldly sorrow fears embarrassment or the loss of reputation. They are like a child who dreads the punishment for their wrongdoing more than true regret for the wrongdoing. Worldly sorrow is lip-service repentance.

Godly sorrow, on the other hand, is a deep remorse for having offended the holy God. It involves a heavy sense of contrition. David describes godly sorrow in the sense of a "broken spirit." He prayed, "You do not delight in sacrifice, or I would bring it; you do not take pleasure in burnt offerings. My sacrifice, O God, is a broken spirit; a broken and contrite heart you, God, will not despise" (Ps. 51:16–17).

Godly sorrow involves genuine confession without covering up a part of our sin, blaming someone else, or rationalizing our actions. True repentance includes the willingness to make restitution whenever possible.

When Thomas was young he and his brother were terrors. Without a dad at home they wandered the streets wreaking havoc. One day, just for the fun of it, they demolished a neighbor's charcoal grill. Years later when Thomas had grown up and committed his life to Christ, he heard a message about what true repentance really meant. He thought about

The power of contrition is the power that drives the gift of recovery.

his past and was moved to right some wrongs. On a Sunday afternoon he went to a store, bought a five-hundred-dollar gas grill and took it to the man whose grill he had destroyed years earlier. The tearful man accepted the grill, but Thomas was the one who experienced the gift of restitution. The funny part of the story is that a few months later, without knowing what Thomas had done, his brother did the same thing! This time the man laughed and said, "Keep the grill. I don't need another one!" The power of contrition drives the gift of recovery.

The Grace of Recovery: Sovereign Appointments

David listened to God and got the word: "Pursue the raiding party!" However, at this point David did not know who the raiding party was. He and his six hundred men set out. On the way God provided the information they needed through an unlikely source.

David and his men found an exhausted Egyptian in a field. They learned the man was an Amalekite slave who had become ill and was left for dead. After giving the Egyptian food and water, the man told them that he had been with the Amalekite raiding party that burned Ziklag. He agreed to lead David and his men to the Amalekites.

An Egyptian who just "happened" to be the slave of an Amalekite who "happened" to get sick and was left behind, who "happened" to be left in the field that David's army was traveling through—God's sovereignty at work. He provided an Amalekite slave, abandoned by his master, to give David all the information needed to find the raiding party. God sovereignly uses people in the grace of recovery process.

I believe that one of the hardest parts of moving out of Ziklag is to admit that you can't do it on your own. After God confronts us and we turn to Him for strength, we can mistake our new spiritual energy for strength of independence. We start to believe that we can recover on our own. Our sinful nature slides back into self-counsel: "No one else needs to know" ... "I can handle the process by myself" ... "My wife and I will work through it" ... "I'll take care of it with the people I've hurt." Such is the insidiousness of sin. Relieved and encouraged by grace, the self-counsel that led us to Ziklag in the first place kicks in again to convince us that we can recover on our own.

However, God has made us for community. Yes, we have Him and yes, He's the One who strengthens us. *And* He made us to need accountability, encouragement, help from others. God strengthened David and provided an Egyptian slave in the grace of recovery.

I have a friend whose marriage survived the sin of adultery. God graciously confronted him and put him on the road to recovery. At times that road has been painful and discouraging, but healing and restoration have taken place. So when I learn of a husband who has been unfaithful, I call my friend and ask him to walk alongside the man on his journey back home. He always says, "You know I hate it that I've been through this experience. But I am thankful that God can use me to help others."

In the same way, we who are soul weary, disillusioned, worn out need the strength and encouragement of others. David's son Solomon tells us that just "as iron sharpens iron, so one person sharpens another" (Prov. 27:17). The grace of recovery moves forward when you are willing to accept the help of the person God sovereignly brings into your life. Solomon further explains this important truth:

> *Two are better than one, because they have a good return for their labor: If either of them falls down, one can help the other up. But pity anyone who falls and has no one to help them up. Also, if two lie down together, they will keep warm. But how can one keep warm alone? Though one may be overpowered, two can defend themselves. A cord of three strands is not quickly broken. (Eccl. 4:9–12)*

The powerful cord of three strands: God. You. And God's sovereign appointment to help you recover.

The Grace of Recovery: Engagement

Life in Ziklag, whether a quick stop, extended stay, or permanent residence, starts with disengaging from God. Soul weariness dries our heart and drives it from the desire for God's presence. Exhausted from service, we ask, "What's the use? Nobody cares," and isolate ourselves from community. Expectations wear us down, so we escape the guilt. ("I am tired of all the service 'opportunities' that I can't live up to.") Disappointment causes us to question God's work in our life and ask, "Why in the world would I be in this situation if God really loved and cared for me?" Enemy territory is filled with the cynical ("Church is filled with a bunch of busybodies") and the disillusioned ("God is irrelevant," "I'm bored with church," "I don't feel like I belong there"). Exhausted. Soul weary. Worn out. We've all been there, but we don't have to stay there. God's grace of recovery allows us to *reengage.*

After God got David's attention with the grace of crisis and provided him with the grace of strength, the king of the Amalekites didn't meet David at the front gate and say, "I am really sorry that I burned your city to the ground and took your wives and children. Here, take your families and all the stuff that is yours. Really, David, I don't know what I was thinking." David had to fight hard to get back what he lost. And so will you. Recovering from spiritual apathy demands engagement with God to put spiritual disciplines in place.

> **Recovering from spiritual apathy demands engagement with God to put spiritual disciplines in place.**

I believe engaging with God involves five spiritual practices. At The Bible Chapel we call these "The Five Essentials."

> **Word.** Engaging with God always begins with reading God's Word. The Bible is His love letter to you. Through the words of Scripture you learn who God is, who you are, how you can know Him intimately, and how you can live for Him. Soul weariness dulls and hardens your heart, but God's Word is like a fire that reignites and like a hammer that breaks through the hard areas (Jer. 23:29).

> **Worship.** Spiritual exhaustion dulls your spiritual emotions. So you need to reengage with a comprehensive

understanding of worship. It is not just a service believers attend. Worship is an active demonstration of your love for God by appropriately responding to His person, work, and Word. Worship is celebrating all God is with all you have and all you are. Worship is all-encompassing and includes an ongoing conversation with God (1 Thess. 5:17). It includes demonstrating your love for God at home, at work, at school, while driving on a busy street, and while standing in a long line at the grocery store. (Why do I always pick the slowest line? So irritating!)

Connect. The Christian life should not be lived solo. As we saw earlier in this chapter, "two are better than one" (Eccl. 4:9). Spiritual fatigue leads you to misread your needs. When you most need others, you may feel a tendency for withdrawal and isolation. Believers must engage with each other for encouragement, support, and prayer.

Serve. In chapter 2 we considered how service can wear us out. And certainly there are times when you need to take a break or back off on too many commitments. But taking a needed break or slowing our pace is different from dropping out of the race. The apostle Peter said that every believer "should use whatever gift you have received to serve others, as faithful stewards of God's grace in its various forms" (1 Peter 4:10). Using the gift(s) that God has given you is energizing when employed in areas of your passion and when you invest realistic amounts of time. Nothing is more satisfying than doing what God has called you to do.

Share. God transformed you from the inside out, made you His child, and set you on a course to eternal life! That's a story that has to be shared. Soul-weary believers are reignited when they tell others what God has done and is doing in their lives. You can even share how God never leaves you, even when you are worn out by obedience! Sharing how God has worked in your life is essential in the grace of recovery.

The revived Egyptian slave took David and his men to the enemy. That's where the battle started, and it was not easy. David and his men fought them from "dusk until the evening of the next day" (1 Sam. 30:17), with pursuit and hand-to-hand combat. Energy was spent and blood was shed. By God's grace David and his men recovered everyone and everything that had been taken. "Nothing was missing: young or old, boy or girl, plunder or anything else they had taken" (1 Sam. 30:19).

The grace of recovery involves a spiritual battle. Satan is the mayor of Ziklag, and he is not a big fan of repentance and recovery. Paul explains that our primary battle "is not against flesh and blood, but against the rulers, against the authorities, against the powers of this dark world and against the spiritual forces of evil in the heavenly realms" (Eph. 6:12). It takes energy and effort to "resist him, standing firm in the faith" (1 Peter 5:9).

The Bible says that sin is fun . . . for a period of time. Ziklag is full of seasonal enjoyment. The grace of recovery engages us in fighting the battle to never return. When you are involved in the battle with addictions, you don't snap your fingers and say, "Cured!" Recovering from consuming debt engages us in the battle of sacrifice and a well-organized budget. Recovering from cynicism calls for a conscious, ongoing effort to grow in gratitude, compassion, and the sure hope of the life Christ gives us.

When you are involved in the battle with addictions, you don't snap your fingers and say, "Cured!"

Don't give up on the people you have hurt. Give them time and space. Allow them to heal. Let them know how sorry you are and how much you desire restoration when they are ready. I know a person who, years after a divorce and remarriage, apologized to his ex-wife. I can't tell you what that meant to her and to their children.

The grace of recovery involves responsibility and effort. It is a battle in which you must engage.

The Grace of Recovery: Receivers Are Givers

When David went out after the enemy, two hundred of his men were too exhausted to continue the pursuit. They were left behind while David and four hundred continued on. These men caught up with the Amalekites, engaged in battle, and reclaimed their wives, children, and plunder. When the victorious soldiers returned they met the men who had stayed behind. Some of David's men said, "Because they did not go out with us, we will not share with them the plunder we recovered. However, each man may take his wife and children and go" (1 Sam. 30:22). But David wouldn't hear of it. He replied:

> *"No, my brothers, you must not do that with what the LORD has given us. He has protected us and delivered into our hands the raiding party that came against us. Who will listen to what you say? The share of the man who stayed with the supplies is to be the same as that of him who went down to the battle. All will share alike." David made this a statute and ordinance for Israel from that day to this.* (1 Sam. 30:23–25)

We who have been freed from sin ought to be the most gracious of people. I am not saying that we should turn a blind eye to sin and disobedience. But Scripture is clear that grace-receivers should be grace-givers.

When I first came to The Bible Chapel I sought to help a family in a difficult situation involving Martha, a godly woman at our church. Her husband was abusive, and the painful circumstance led to separation in order to protect the family. A protection from abuse order was issued for protection at home and our elders kept him from coming into the church building when the family was there. Hatred built in the hearts of the two older boys. At times they wanted to kill their stepfather. The two younger children were deeply affected emotionally.

After years of legal protection and separation, Martha's ex-husband was diagnosed with terminal cancer. By God's grace the family ministered to him during his illness and was at his bedside when he passed away. Martha wrote, "During that time I witnessed each of my four children reaching out to him and saw amazing forgiveness by his two stepsons—it went as far as words of love to him. During that time God opened my ex-husband's heart . . . he truly was a troubled saint, a broken man. Basically, we forgave my ex-husband and served him even though the world would say, 'He didn't deserve it.' Hey, none of us deserve His mercy; but He sure gave us mercy through His Son."

Peter, Martha's second-oldest son, said, "I didn't honor him, I wanted to kill him. It wasn't until I matured in my faith and was not under his control anymore that I was able to see him from God's eyes. Forgiving him as Christ forgave me removed the rage . . . and allowed me to see the broken, hurting man that he was. Then to witness the greatest example of love that I've ever seen, my mother taking care of her ex-husband (my stepfather) on his deathbed and watching God work on this man's heart again . . . to see [our] mother loving and caring for [her ex-husband] to the end. The value in watching this cannot be measured. In fact, it impacted everyone that's ever known our family."

The apostle Paul instructed the Ephesian believers to "be kind and compassionate to one another, forgiving each other, just as in Christ God forgave you" (Eph. 4:32). When God graciously rescues us we must show that same grace to others.

Grace of Recovery: Saved from What Could Have Been

Remember David's story. His years of running from Saul took a toll. Twice David had the opportunity to end the chase but, in obedience, refused to kill God's anointed king. While in Ziklag,

David raided Israel's enemies instead of the Philistine enemies. Then, in an amazing turn of events, David lined up with the Philistines to fight the Israelites.

God graciously moved in the hearts of four of the Philistine kings who feared that David would turn on them during the battle. Even though David argued to join the fight, they refused to let him engage against the Israelites. It was after the Philistine kings' rejection that David and his men returned to Ziklag, found the city burned, and discovered their families had been taken captive.

The Philistines continued their plan to encounter Israel. In that engagement, Saul and his sons were killed. From the battlefield a servant delivered Saul's crown to David, and he became Israel's king. God graciously kept David from that battle.

The grace of recovery sometimes is the grace of *protection*— saving us from what could have happened. If you have never been to Ziklag, you of all people should be thankful for God's grace. We all know our propensities and weaknesses. God's grace keeps us from what could have been.

God will graciously lead us to recover from our time in Zikag. But *staying* out of Ziklag will depend on our acceptance and understanding of who we are—or better, whose we are. Spiritual identity trumps all the difficult circumstances of life . . . even soul weariness. That's what we'll see in the next chapter.

Reflect

1. Consider Olivia's story at the beginning of this chapter. What aspects of her story can you relate to?

2. Review the section on repentance in this chapter. As you reflect, what are the essential components of true repentance? Which ones are most difficult for you to accept?

3. Explain the difference between worldly sorrow and godly sorrow. How can you determine if you have truly embraced godly sorrow?

4. It is often difficult to ask others to walk with us on our road back home. But why is it important to have a strong believer join us on the journey to recovery?

5. Why is forgiving others critical in the grace of recovery?

CHAPTER 10

SPIRITUAL IDENTITY: WHOSE AM I?

*The fact that I was going into this event knowing that
my identity is rooted in Christ and not the result of this
competition just gave me peace . . . and it let me enjoy
the contest. If something went great, I was happy.
If something didn't go great, I could still find joy.*[1]
—STEELE JOHNSON, OLYMPIC DIVER

As I mentioned earlier, the sermon series this book
is based on resonated deeply with those who attend our
church. The opportunity to make the message of David's experience—and ours—available to a larger audience has been an
answered prayer. And . . . the process has been exhausting.

The first deadline for the book was in the fall, which provided
an opportunity for me to secure blocks of time to write during
the summer months. But due to a variety of factors beyond
anyone's control, the deadline was moved to the first of the
year. This meant the heavy lifting of the writing process had to

be done during the fall and holiday seasons. A new sermon series in the fall absorbed time for study and prep, as did teaching a class for parents on Wednesday evenings. Extra elders' meetings were needed as we made plans for a three-year re-visioning effort. As I dealt with staff, interacted with people on normal pastoral issues, preached most weekends through the fall, delivered five Christmas Eve messages, and prepared and spoke at a six-day conference in another country, I began experiencing the very thing I was writing about.

My levels of cynicism began to rise, and my spiritual emotions flatlined. I became soul weary.

This has happened to me before, and it will happen again. But for me, everything I have described above is my calling and vocation. However, many of you reading this minister at your job—and then, on top of that, use your spiritual gifts and energies to serve the church.

Take Mark, Bob, and Devin. They scheduled a meeting with me to discuss some concerns. These guys are movers and shakers in the Pittsburgh real estate development world and major players on our church's building team. In an eighteen-month stretch they oversaw the planning and construction of an addition to our largest campus, the construction of a new facility for another campus, the refurbishing of an older facility we purchased for a third campus, and the evaluation of a building for a campus we were getting ready to launch. They sat down in my office and said, "We are exhausted!" These men, whose normal workweek is sixty-plus hours, were adding another ten to fifteen a week to serve the church . . . and they were spent. Even movers and shakers born with a type-A personality and "git-'er-done" DNA can become worn out by obedience.

As we have seen through this book, soul weariness, delivered by nagging temptations, overcommitted service, the weight of expectations, and the inevitable disappointments of life, hits us all. If this weariness is left unchecked, we are in danger of a move to Ziklag to take a short break from God or disconnect from Him altogether. We thank God for His grace that moves us out of Ziklag—but larger questions remain. Is there a way to stay away from Ziklag, or at least make it an infrequent destination?

Remember playing tag as a kid? You would run around the playground or the backyard, escaping from the person who was "it." Somewhere in the parameters of the game there was always a "base," where you could remain safe from the person who was "it." Like the person who is "it" in the game of tag, soul weariness chases the believer through life. We need a base—a place to stay safe and protected. That base is Jesus, and all believers find their spiritual identity in Him. Understanding our spiritual identity—whose we are—is the remedy for spiritual fatigue. In Christ we are SSAFE: Significant. Secure. Accepted. Forgiven. Empowered.

The Base: Spiritual Identity

The Bourne movie (and book) series are action spy thrillers based on the adventures of fictional CIA agent Jason Bourne. The movies are packed with intense drama, crazy chases, and Bourne jumping from the roof of one high-rise building to another in order to escape those trying to end his life. Bourne is trained and equipped, a fighting machine with astonishing intellect. But due to extreme memory loss he can't remember who he is. Throughout the series Jason Bourne searches for his true identity.

In the first movie, *The Bourne Identity,* Bourne sits in a roadside café confused and reflective. Looking out the window he says:

> I can tell you the license plate numbers of all six cars outside. I can tell you that our waitress is left-handed and the guy sitting up at the counter weighs two hundred and fifteen pounds and knows how to handle himself. I know the best place to look for a gun is the cab of the gray truck outside, and at this altitude, I can run flat out for a half mile before my hands start shaking. Now why would I know that? How can I know that and not know who I am?[2]

Many of us are like Jason Bourne. Our head is full of Christian knowledge. We know the Bible stories and can find our way around Scripture. With some effort, we can even locate the Old Testament book of Nahum! We can explain to others what it means to become a Christian and how to grow in our relationship with Christ. Still, our minds echo with Bourne's question: *How can I know all that and not know who I am?* And when we feel that way, when we begin to deal with that question, we can be vulnerable to the detour that leads to Ziklag. In order for believers to effectively move from knowledge to deal with spiritual struggles, we must have a clear understanding of our spiritual identity in Christ.

Before life with Jesus our question was, "Who am I?" as we sought to find meaning and purpose within our pursuits and ourselves. Now our life in Christ flips the question from "Who am I?" to "Whose am I?" That question is answered in the person of Jesus. Followers of Christ become a new creation with a new identity, described through the words of the prophet Isaiah, "Do not fear, for I have redeemed you; I have summoned you by name; *you are mine*" (43:1b, emphasis added). We belong to Jesus!

When we feel soul weariness coming on, our position in Christ needs to be tucked away as the underpinning of our soul. This truth forms the foundation to which we cling and find rest.

In Christ I Am SIGNIFICANT

Until it failed to pass inspection, I drove an old, beat-up car with rusty fenders, a veteran of many Pittsburgh winters, battered from being driven by our four children. The car had many . . . issues. Each time I took it in to a friend's shop for more work, he said, "When are you going to get rid of this thing!" I have to admit that I was a little embarrassed to drive the car. Each time I pulled up to a stoplight I wanted to roll my window down and say, "Hey, don't look at me like that. I'm about ready to trade this car in for a newer one, one that will make me feel more significant."

It's crazy, isn't it? We look to things of the world—cars, houses, positions, titles, etc.—to make us feel significant. But the things of the world never satisfy our soul; they only wear it out. The truth of God's Word must frame our significance, found only in Christ.

We are made in the image of God. The eternal God made us in His image (Gen. 1:26–27), gave us life, and provided us with ability to learn, retain knowledge, create life, and through Christ, live forever.

We have been redeemed. God purchased us and set us free from the control of sin. He rescued us "from the dominion of darkness and brought us into the kingdom of the Son he loves, in whom we have redemption, the forgiveness of sins" (Col. 1:13–14).

We have been transformed. In Christ we are a new creation, the old is in the past; the new is here (2 Cor. 5:17).

Our significance does not depend on "who I am" but "whose I am." God's work on our behalf makes us significant. This is a truth that supersedes soul weariness. Our significance is not based on how we feel, what we are going through, our appearance, or our position. Ken Boa says it this way:

> We are constantly in danger of letting the world instead of God define us, because that is so easy to do. It is only natural to shape our self-image by the attitudes and opinions of our parents, our peer groups, and our society. None of us are immune to the distorting effects of performance-based acceptance, and we can falsely conclude that we are worthless or that we must try to earn God's acceptance. Only when we define ourselves by the truths of the Word rather than the thinking and experiences of the world can we discover our deepest identity.[4]

In Christ I Am SECURE

I became a Christian when I was around twelve years old, and my family was very involved in our small church. The fellowship was meaningful. The worship was uplifting. The messages were based on the Bible and applicable. But there were challenges with the church's doctrine. I was taught that Christians could lose their salvation, that an act of sin severed one's relationship with God. I grew up believing that I could be headed for heaven in the morning, then sin at lunch and be on my way to hell by the afternoon.

Then one day, in a first-year seminary class, my eyes were opened to the truth of God's Word regarding the security of my relationship with Jesus. I remember contemplating the truth as I walked to my car after class. There in a hot parking lot in Dallas the truth finally sank in. I was a child of God and would forever be! Nothing could ever separate me from His love! I felt a load lifted from my shoulders as I realized that I was secure in Christ. For the first time I understood that God's love for me was not based on my performance.

God's love for us is complete and perfect! There is nothing we can do to make Him love us more; there is nothing we can do to make Him love us less. Our security is not based on what we have done, but on what Jesus has done for us.

We have been justified. Justification is a legal term with two eternal benefits. God, the holy Judge, applied the work of His Son to us. The debt of our sin is paid in full by Jesus' work on the cross. God declares us "Not Guilty!" and "Righteous!" (see Rom. 3:22–24).

God's love for us is unconditional. Nothing can separate us from the heavenly Father. In one of my favorite passages Paul explained that nothing "in all creation, will be able to separate us from the love of God that is in Christ Jesus our Lord" (Rom. 8:38–39).

We are protected. In his letter to the Christians in Colossae, the apostle Paul explained that all believers are "hidden with Christ in God" (Col. 3:3). Jesus is our refuge and hiding place.[5]

Our position is sealed. In the days of the New Testament, when you wanted to send a letter or document, you folded the paper and poured wax over the fold. Each family had a ring designed with its special sign. The sender pushed the ring into the wax leaving the unique mark. Seals were marks of identification, authenticity, and security. When the carrier delivered the envelope, the recipient could determine who sent the document and could make sure the seal was genuine. If the seal was unbroken, the recipient knew that the contents were secure. In Christ, God puts His "seal of ownership" on every believer (2 Cor. 1:21–22).

We will pass from death to life. Jesus promises that when those who follow Him die, they will "cross[ ] over" from death to life (John 5:24). There is no purgatory, holding stage, or soul sleep. When we are absent from the body, we will be present with the Lord (2 Cor. 5:6–8). That's security!

In Christ I Am ACCEPTED

Luis is an orphan who lives in Panama. He never knew his biological parents. He was abandoned early on and moved from one state-run orphanage to another. When a family tragically lost their son, they decided to adopt Luis to take their son's place. As you can imagine, that didn't work.

When the adoptive parents realized that Luis could not replace their son, they dropped him off at the Panamanian equivalent to Children and Youth Services. Luis was placed into a Christian transition home, supported by our church. He had never experienced true acceptance. Every day for more than a year the house parents had to assure him, "Luis, we are not sending you back today!"[6]

God has adopted and accepted us into His family. Paul wrote, "But when the set time had fully come, God sent his Son, born of a woman, born under the law, to redeem those under the law, that we might receive adoption to sonship" (Gal. 4:4–5). Adoption provides full acceptance. It grants all the privileges of natural-born children, including inheritance rights. In Christ we are accepted. Paul explains, "So you are no longer a slave, but God's child; and since you are his child, God has made you also an heir" (Gal. 4:7). Every day God tells us, "You are My child. I am not sending you back!"

Some believers will wear themselves out trying to be accepted in the "right" group. Some will risk their reputations and abandon their values to keep the company of the cool crowd (even the cool Christian crowd). But being a people-pleaser will wear you out. You don't have to perform for people; you are a child and eternal heir of the King of kings!

In Christ I Am FORGIVEN

The guilt of sin is a heavy burden to carry. It impacts us physically as well as spiritually. When David lived with unrepentant sin, he felt as if his strength was being sapped "as in the heat of summer" (Ps. 32:4). But God's forgiveness brings relief from guilt's burden.

In the Hebrew language of the Old Testament, the primary word translated "forgive" (*nasa*) means to "lift, carry, or take."

It has the idea of lifting something off a person and carrying it away. In the Greek language of the New Testament, two main words are translated "forgive." The Greek word *aphiemi* means "to let go or cancel." Another word used often is *aphesis*. It means "to release or pardon."

Only through God's forgiveness can we finally let go of past guilt. C. S. Lewis wrote, "I think that if God forgives us we must forgive ourselves. Otherwise it is almost like setting up ourselves as a higher tribunal than Him."[7] If you are struggling with sin—its present weight or the guilt of the past—take some time to ask God to help you experience His full and complete forgiveness. Pray the promises of the following passages.

> *Surely it was for my benefit that I suffered such anguish. In your love you kept me from the pit of destruction; you have put all my sins behind your back. (Isa. 38:17)*

> *For I will forgive their wickedness and will remember their sins no more. (Jer. 31:34)*

> *Who is a God like you, who pardons sin and forgives the transgression of the remnant of his inheritance? You do not stay angry forever but delight to show mercy. You will again have compassion on us; you will tread our sins underfoot and hurl all our iniquities into the depths of the sea. (Micah 7:18–19)*

> *For as high as the heavens are above the earth, so great is his love for those who fear him; as far as the east is from the west, so far has he removed our transgressions from us. (Ps. 103:11–12)*

Living with the guilt of sin is exhausting. It is like having several programs open on our computer. Even when we are not using the program it drains the power and slows the computer's speed. But forgiveness brings relief. Jerry Bridges says, "The assurance of [God's] total forgiveness of our sins through the blood of Christ means we don't have to play defensive games anymore. We don't have to rationalize and excuse our sins. We can call sin exactly what it is, regardless of how ugly and shameful it may be, because we know that Jesus bore that sin in His body on the cross."[8] Forgiveness brings freedom with God.

One more—and important—point concerning forgiveness. Many Christians who understand and accept God's forgiveness of them refuse to forgive others. Unforgiveness and the accompanying bitterness will wear you out. It's time to extend to others the forgiveness that God has extended to you (Eph. 4:32).

In Christ I Am EMPOWERED

The moment we become a believer the Holy Spirit takes up residence in our heart (John 14:17). The Spirit counsels and convicts us (John 16:13). He teaches and transforms us (John 16:12–14; 2 Cor. 5:17). The Spirit secures our relationship with Jesus, giving assurance that we belong to Christ (Eph. 1:13–14; Rom. 8:15–16). When we experience those exhausting times and can't find words to pray, the Holy Spirit takes over and prays on our behalf (Rom. 8:26–27). These are all things the Spirit does for us—and there is one more thing that we do in partnership with the Spirit.

In Ephesians 5:18, Paul writes, "Do not get drunk on wine which leads to debauchery. Instead, be filled with the Spirit."

...e word *filled* means to be controlled. Alcohol, in excess, is a controlling substance. Too much alcohol blurs our vision, slurs our speech, slows our reaction, and skews our perception. Paul commands the believer to a control of a different kind. The Greek word translated *be filled* is in the imperative voice, which means it is something we must do. The word is also in the present tense, calling for continuous application. We must continually ask the Holy Spirit to control our life.

The Holy Spirit empowers us, providing everything needed to do what God is calling us to do. We cannot live the Christian life on our own. The believer's strength must come from the Holy Spirit.

Following is a prayer that will help you submit to the Spirit's control. This is a request that you can pray throughout the day.

> *Father, this is Your day on loan to me and I want to be used by You for eternal and lasting purposes. I submit myself, my plans, my activities, and my interactions with others to You. I thank You that I have been baptized and sealed by Your Spirit. I thank You that Your Spirit indwells me. Now I ask that Your Spirit control every aspect of my life. Take control of my tongue that my words will reflect Your love and grace. Take control of my emotions that I may respond obediently and calmly. Take control of my thoughts that my mind may be quickly cleaned of those things that will not honor You and be full of things that are true, noble, right, pure, lovely, and praiseworthy. Control my actions in such a way that others will see my deeds and know that they have been influenced by You. Give me the strength to live this day in*

*a way that pleases You. I submit myself to Your control in
Christ's name. Amen.*

The Holy Spirit lives within you. He will provide all you
need to do all that God has called you to do. Through the power
of the Holy Spirit you can deal with soul weariness and stay far
from the detours to Ziklag.

The Freedom of Identity

After participating in the 2008 Olympic games in Beijing, US
diver David Boudia hit a wall. The Purdue student felt purpose-
less and even contemplated suicide. In his desperate state, he
reached out to his college coach, Adam Soldati, and Soldati's
wife, Kimiko. It was through them that Boudia trusted in Jesus
Christ. Boudia explained it this way:

> *Through Adam's faithful friendship in ministering the
> Word to me, I came to know Christ. I began to be discipled
> in my walk with Christ. I also sought out biblical counseling.
> Slowly and not always consistently, I began to realize from
> the Word of God that my purpose in life as God's child was
> to live for Him and others—not myself. Living for David's
> fame and David's pleasure was one of my biggest problems
> in the 2008 Beijing Olympics and was the cause of my
> deepest moments of despair.*[9]

After winning gold and bronze medals at the 2012 London
Olympics Boudia said that he had found something even more
valuable. He said, "God was completely sovereign throughout

this entire journey. He knew how it was going to happen, when it was going to happen, and we know why it happens—to make me more like Christ."[10]

Following their silver medal performance in the men's synchronized ten meter platform at the 2016 Rio Olympic games, David stood with his diving partner, Steele Johnson, to be interviewed. When asked by NBC reporter Kelli Stavast, "What does it mean to come out and medal here in the synchro event?" Boudia responded.

> Yeah, I just think the past week, there's just been an enormous amount of pressure, and I've felt it. You know, it's just an identity crisis. When my mind is on this, thinking I'm defined by this, then my mind goes crazy, but we both know our identity is in Christ.[11]

Steele Johnson added that knowing Christ gave him peace going into the competition. He said:

> The way David just described it was flawless—the fact that I was going into this event knowing that my identity is rooted in Christ and not the result of this competition just gave me peace ... and it let me enjoy the contest. If something went great, I was happy. If something didn't go great, I could still find joy.[12]

Just like an Olympic diver, we can feel tremendous pressure to receive high scores for obedience. We live with an internal desire to please Jesus and are disappointed in ourselves when we fail. We also desire to demonstrate our love by our actions and too often can slip into a performance mentality. The internal disappointment and external performance can wear us down. But . . . our identity is in Jesus. In Him we will always be significant whether our day scores are "10's" or "3's." In Christ we are significant. The Father loved us so much that He sent His Son to die for our sins. In Christ we are always secure; nothing can separate us from His love. In Christ we are always accepted. Our Father loves us with a perfect, unconditional love. In Christ we are forgiven. Our sins are wiped clean. In Christ we are empowered. Through the Holy Spirit we have everything we need to do what God calls us to do.

When Lori and I lived in Dallas, construction started behind our apartments on a multistory office building. In the evenings I'd walk over to the construction site and looked through openings in a tall fence surrounding the entire project. Initially what I saw was nothing more than a big hole in the ground. But over the next few months the building started taking shape. That big hole in the ground rose hundreds of feet into the sky—a significant structure!

You are so significant to God that He is in the process of building you. Sometimes it is hard to find significance in the midst of the process. But remember, your significance is found in the fact that God is at work in your life, stretching you and molding you into His masterpiece. It seems like a struggle, but remember, God is always working in you—as Paul says, "being confident of this, that he who began a good work in you will carry it on to completion until the day of Christ Jesus" (Phil. 1:6).

Reflect

1. What do you want people to think about when they hear your name? Beautiful? Handsome? Rich? Smart? Clever? Funny? Hard worker? Humble? Powerful? Popular? Athletic? Musical? Self-starter? Go-getter? Reserved? Thoughtful? Reflective? Problem solver? All the above?

2. What defines you? Appearance? Style? What you drive? Profession? Address? Titles? Degrees? Money? Friends? Hobby? Sports team? Recreation? Travel? Past? Dreams? Future plans? Job? Accomplishments? Motherhood? Fatherhood? Service?

3. What drives you? Grades? Career? Advancement? Goals? Acceptance? Relationships? Retirement? A certain lifestyle? Sexuality? Portfolio? Awards?

4. Describe a time when you experienced the freedom of forgiveness.

CHAPTER 11

THE LORD WHO BURSTS THROUGH

He reached down from heaven and rescued me; he drew me out of deep waters. —PSALM 18:16 NLT

My wife, Lori, and I grew up in Perry, Oklahoma—a small town located in the north-central part of the state. In Perry, the sport of wrestling is king. The Perry Maroons boast one of the most successful high school wrestling programs in the United States, having won 40 state championships since 1952 and producing over 150 individual state champions.

When I was growing up, wrestling started in the fifth grade, but my brother was a friend of the coach so I got to start in the third grade (lucky me!). The peewee wrestlers practiced in an old classroom of the high school with a white vinyl mat on the floor. Each day we would run, do exercises, learn new holds and moves, and wrestle with a person our weight and size. I was doing fine, even enjoying some success as a third-grader, until one fateful Friday afternoon. For some reason, my usual partner did not show up for practice.

As I looked around the room that day, the only other person who did not have a partner was a boy named Edward. My heart sank. Edward was big and mean. The word on the street was, "Stay away from Edward!" Edward was in the sixth grade . . . for the second or third time. Edward had a full beard in the sixth grade. When he saw that I was without a partner, a big grin crossed his bearded face and he headed my way. At that point I lost control of my bodily functions.

The next thirty minutes are burned into my memory even today. Edward owned me. He busted my lip in several places. He pinned my back to the mat several times. He severely wounded my little ego. All these decades later I still remember getting up from my most recent pinning, walking to a combination sink and water fountain, spitting blood into the sink, getting a drink and thinking, "Oh boy! I get to go back out there again. Edward— the half-man, half-animal—is going to pin me repeatedly until practice is over." I spent that day on my back, down on the mat, worn out by Edward.

In this book we have discussed those things that wear us down and keep us down. We have considered what drives us to make quick trips or short visits to Ziklag, or settle in for extended stays. My plea to you as we end our journey together is to stay far away from Ziklag. If you are in Ziklag I beg you to ask Jesus to help pack your bags and leave.

The prophet Micah knew what it was like to fall, but he refused to stay down. He wrote, "Do not gloat over me, my enemy! Though I have fallen, I will rise" (Micah 7:8). With

Micah you can say, *Do not gloat over me, my enemy! Satan, you are my enemy and you delight in my failure. But if you think I will stay down, think again! Though I have fallen, I will rise! Yes, I have spent too much time in Ziklag, pinned down by the enemy and too weary to get up. But today through the power of the Holy Spirit, I will rise!*

I want to close with Kathleen's story—a young millennial who experienced life in Ziklag for seven years but by God's grace packed her bags and moved home. If you are in Ziklag, I pray that Kathleen's story becomes yours.

12/30/2015 is a date written in my Bible and next to it are the words "I am free." Free and saved after seven years drowning in the deep waters of Ziklag.

Ziklag is not a place you suddenly decide to go; it is a quiet and gradual journey in the opposite direction of where you want to be and away from the One to whom you belong. For me, Ziklag became a life of using the world to fill the parts of me that felt empty. My lifestyle was not blatant, which allowed me to live a "successful" double life for many years.

The years in Ziklag produced waves—waves of guilt, conviction, and efforts to leave; waves of complete indifference and indulgence. I felt hopeless and intensely aware of my inability to ever get out.

Early on I made my first attempt to escape Ziklag. I left, but it didn't last. I went back. I felt fake and insincere and questioned if I even wanted to leave. The satisfaction my sins offered me, albeit brief and superficial, had become my new addiction. It was reliable and constant. I could depend on the temporary high, and I grew accustomed to dealing with the inevitable lows.

Returning to Ziklag so quickly was all Satan needed to fully convince me that I was not ever going to leave. He worked fast at replacing any truth I had left with lies, and soon I believed them completely. I turned sin into more sin. I dove in deeper this time. I gave up on trying to leave. If I failed once, I would most certainly fail again.

At this point the unrest (of being so far away from the Lord) became compounded by a new feeling of mourning. I daily mourned the loss of the life I once had and the life I wanted back. I grieved, believing that the future I always imagined was now impossible. Everything the Lord had for me was gone, and not only could I no longer see it, but I was purposefully running further and further from it.

If there is one thing I learned about successfully living a double life of sin in the land of the enemy, it was that you must push away anyone that threatens that. And that is exactly what I did. I lied and worked very hard to make sure my life looked neat and "in order." To Christians (and especially to my family), I replied "fine" to any questions, making sure they knew nothing about the life I was living.

It has now been a year since the Lord rescued me from Ziklag. I did not wake up one morning and decide to try again. I had been there for seven years. I had no plans to leave. It was my life. But the Lord had other plans. "'The LORD did it,' David exclaimed. 'He burst through my enemies like a raging flood.' So he named that place Baal-perazim (which means 'the Lord who bursts through')" (2 Samuel 5:20 NLT). My life was suddenly interrupted. In an intricate plan, the Lord used a course of everyday events, situations, and people over a matter of mere days to (what felt like literally) reach down and pull me into His arms, saying, "It's time to leave!" I was rescued. I was shown utmost grace. This was not my doing, because I was weak and incapable. This was God. This was God chasing after me and doing for me what I could have never done for myself.

The same day God "burst through," I did something I vowed I would never do. I went to the one person that knew nothing of my life in Ziklag—the one person that prayed for me every single day. I went to my mother and told her where I had been for the last seven years. The secret was out and I vividly remember thinking, "I don't feel like I am dying anymore." I needed her. I needed someone to walk with me. Doing this on my own was not an option. I had tried that and failed.

The sense of freedom was overwhelming. Something had been lifted. But just as overwhelming as this freedom was the sense of preparation for battle. Yes, God had intervened but this was not going to be easy. Serious changes had to be made. People were cut off. There were places I would never go again. Phone numbers deleted. I met with a counselor weekly. I checked in with my mom and a close friend daily. And I spent every night for many months sobbing on the floor before the Lord. I sobbed out of exhaustion. Those days were undoubtedly the hardest and most important. You don't just pick up your things and start a new life. I cried out and pleaded to the Lord to give me strength. But even more than this, I sobbed out of complete gratitude and HOPE, unable to understand why the Lord would come after me. How a Father could love me so much after what I had done. And it is this HOPE and LOVE that keeps me going today. Every single day is the choice to accept and depend on the Lord's strength to continue moving forward. It is not *easy, but it is possible through Him. And while there are still days that I fear I will fail, HE has never failed me yet. And that, I have learned, is all I need.*

A year ago I thought Ziklag was my future. Today it is a memory that amazingly feels more distant with each day. I am confident today that God is going to use those years for His purpose and glory. I see His hand in them despite how far away I was. I see how He spared me. I see how He protected me from innumerable conse-quences. I see how He never let me go. Yes, God burst in and saved me on that day, but He continues to save me every single day, and for that I rejoice and praise Him every single day.

Kathleen's Ziklag story is one of leaving and returning, success and failure, hope and despair, but most of all it is a story of God's amazing love, power, and grace. He is the "Lord who bursts through!" He is ready to burst through your "enemies," pick you up off the mat, pack your bags, and rescue you from Ziklag. Kathleen's story is powerful! I can't wait to hear yours.

NOTES

Introduction

1. Greg Hawkins and Sally Parkinson, "Reveal: Spiritual Life Survey Report—The Bible Chapel Composite" (Willow Creek Association: unpublished survey, June 2012).

Chapter 1: Running on Empty

1. Quoted in Leonardo Blair, "Cross Point Church Senior Pastor Pete Wilson Resigns, Tells Congregation 'I'm Tired . . . Broken,'" *Christian Post*, September 12, 2016, http://www.christianpost.com/news/cross-point-church-senior-pastor-pete-wilson-resigns-tells-congregation-im-tired-broken-169465/.
2. Jerry Bridges, *The Pursuit of Holiness* (Colorado Springs: NavPress, 1978), 13–14.
3. Quoted in Blair, "Pastor Pete Wilson Resigns."

Chapter 3: Worn Out by Expectations

1. Dan Patrick, "Just My Type: The Interview," *Sports Illustrated*, February 21, 2011, www.si.com/vault/2011/02/21/106038173/just-my-type.
2. Ibid.
3. Dan B. Allender and Tremper Longman III, *Intimate Allies* (Wheaton, IL: Tyndale, 1995), 28.
4. Ibid., 303.

Chapter 4: Worn Out by Disappointment

1. Matthew Henry, *Matthew Henry's Commentary On the Whole Bible* (Peabody, MA: Hendrickson Publishers, 1991), vol. 2, 333.

Chapter 5: My Own Worst Counselor

1. Tony Parsons, "Bowie, What Is He Like?" on *Exploring David Bowie*, February 13, 2013, https://exploringdavidbowie.wordpress.com/2013/02/14/bowie-what-is-he-like/.
2. Douglas Martin, "Roger Boisjoly, 73, Dies; Warned of Shuttle Danger," *New York Times*, February 3, 2012, http://www.nytimes.com/2012/02/04/us/roger-boisjoly-73-dies-warned-of-shuttle-danger.html.
3. BBC News, "David Bowie: Friends and Stars Pay Tribute," news release, January 11, 2016, http://www.bbc.com/news/entertainment-arts-35279642.

4. Parsons, "Bowie, What Is He Like?"

5. Anthony DeCurtis, *In Other Words: Artists Talk About Life and Work* (Milwaukee, WI: Hal Leonard, 2005), 262–63.

6. BBC News, "Rock Star David Bowie Leaves $100m in Will," news release, January 30, 2016, http://www.bbc.com/news/entertainment-arts-35449063.

7. Parsons, "Bowie, What Is He Like?"

8. Ron Moore, *Living Grounded: Embracing the Foundational Truths of the Christian Faith* (McMurray, PA: The Journey Ministry, 2015), 35.

9. Eugene Peterson, *A Long Obedience in the Same Direction: Discipleship in an Instant Society* (Downers Grove, IL: InterVarsity Press, 1980), 51.

Chapter 6: Into Enemy Territory

1. Fyodor Dostoyevsky, *The Brothers Karamazov*, trans. Constance Garnett (New York: Barnes and Noble, 1995), 37.

2. See also Galatians 6:7–9 and 1 Timothy 5:24.

3. Dostoyevsky, *Brothers Karamazov*, 37.

4. Robert B. Chisholm, Jr., "Joel," in *The Bible Knowledge Commentary Old Testament: An Exposition of the Scriptures,* ed. John F. Walvoord and Roy B. Zuck (Wheaton, IL: Victor, 1985), 1420.

Chapter 7: The Grace of Crisis

1. Dietrich Bonhoeffer, *Creation and Fall and Temptation* (New York: Touchstone, 1997), 132.

Chapter 8: The Grace of Strength

1. Charles R. Swindoll, *Flying Closer to the Flame* (Dallas: Word, 1993), 27.

2. Alister McGrath, *Mere Apologetics* (Grand Rapids: 2012), 167.

3. Ibid., 170.

4. Simon Guillebaud, *For What It's Worth* (Oxford: Lion Hudson, 1999), 171; cited in Simon Wenham, "Is Christianity a Crutch?," Ravi Zacharias International Ministries, March 21, 2013, rzim.org/a-slice-of-infinity/is-christianity-a-crutch.

5. Swindoll, *Flying Closer to the Flame,* 26–27.

Chapter 9: The Grace of Recovery

1. "The Mediator," in *The Valley of Vision: A Collection of Puritan Prayers and Devotions,* ed. Arthur Bennett (Carlisle, PA: The Banner of Truth Trust, 1975), 40.

Chapter 10: Spiritual Identity: Whose Am I?

1. Jonah Hicap, "US Diving Duo David Boudia and Steele Johnson Proclaim Christ on TV after Bagging Olympic Silver," *World*, August 9, 2016, http://www.christiantoday.com/article/us.diving.duo .david.boudia.and.steele.johnson.proclaim.christ.on.tv.after.bagging .olympic.silver/92711.htm.

2. *The Bourne Identity*, directed by Doug Liman, Universal Pictures, 2004, DVD.

3. Three Greek words are used in the New Testament to explain what it means to be redeemed. The word *agoraz* means "to purchase" (2 Peter 2:1; Rev. 5:9). The word *exagorazi* means "to purchase out of the marketplace." Spiritually speaking, this means "to purchase out of the marketplace of sin" (Gal. 3:13; 4:5). The word *lutroo* means "to release and set free" (1 Tim. 2:6; Titus 2:14).

4. Kenneth Boa, *Conformed to His Image* (Grand Rapids: Zondervan, 2001), 35.

5. Norman L. Geisler, "Colossians," in *The Bible Knowledge Commentary New Testament: An Exposition of the Scriptures,* ed. John F. Walvoord and Roy B. Zuck (Wheaton, IL: Victor Books, 1985), 680.

6. Ron Moore, *Living Grounded: Embracing the Foundational Truths of the Christian Faith* (McMurray, PA: The Journey Ministry, 2015), 87.

7. C. S. Lewis, April 19, 1951, letter to Miss Breckenridge in *The Collected Letters of C. S. Lewis*, vol. 3, ed. Walter Hooper (San Francisco: Harper-Collins, 2007), 109.

8. Jerry Bridges, *The Discipline of Grace* (Colorado Springs: NavPress, 1994), 22–23.

9. Daniel S. Levine, "David Boudia's Faith: 5 Fast Facts You Need to Know," *Heavy*, August 8, 2016, http://heavy.com/sports/2016/08/ david-boudia-faith-christianity-rio-olympics-team-usa-diving-soonie-family-adam-soldati-what-is/.

10. Ibid.

11. Michael Morris, "US Olympic Divers Following Silver Medal Performance: 'Our Identity Is in Christ,' *CNS News,* August 9, 2016, http:// www.cnsnews.com/blog/michael-morris/us-olympic-divers-following-silver-medal-performance-our-identity-christ.

12. Hicap, "US Diving Duo."

ACKNOWLEDGMENTS

Thanks . . .

To Phil Rawley who believed in this project from the beginning and pursued the right people at Moody Publishers.

To Duane Sherman and all of the other Moody Publishers people who gave their enthusiastic support to this project. Working with you has been a pleasure.

To Betsey Newenhuyse who patiently and skillfully combed the manuscript to cut, edit, advise, and prompt new thinking through this entire project. You are truly gifted and your input has been greatly appreciated.

To my wife, Lori, who reads, critiques, edits, and molds everything I write. Thank you for believing in this project. And to all of our children, Brittany and Josiah, Garrison and Sarah, Lara and DJ, and Mackenzie, who provided needed and helpful input along the way.

To Maria Stockman who gave needed feedback from the beginning and also helped with the technical aspects of the draft.

To the congregation of The Bible Chapel whose encouragement, love, and support over twenty-five years of ministry has allowed me and my family to stay in one spot and see the fruit of longevity. This book is filled with your stories.

ABOUT THE AUTHOR

Ron Moore is the Senior Pastor of The Bible Chapel, a multisite church in Pittsburgh, PA. He serves as President and Bible Teacher of Back to the Bible. Ron earned his Master of Theology and Doctor of Ministry degrees from Dallas Theological Seminary. He has a passion to see people develop as followers of Jesus Christ. He is the author of several books including *Ignite: Sparking a Heart That Burns for God*, *Unshakable: Rock-Solid Faith*, and *Refuge: Devotions for Finding Strength and Comfort*. For more information, visit backtothebible.org or biblechapel.org.

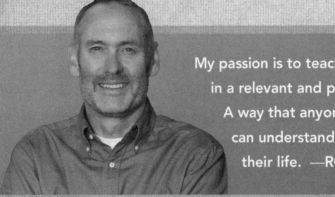
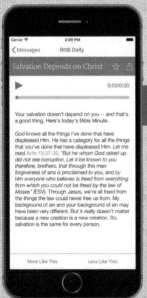

SOONER OR LATER, JUST LIKE THE REST OF US, YOU'LL ASK **THE QUESTION:**
WHY, GOD? WHY DID YOU LET THIS HAPPEN?

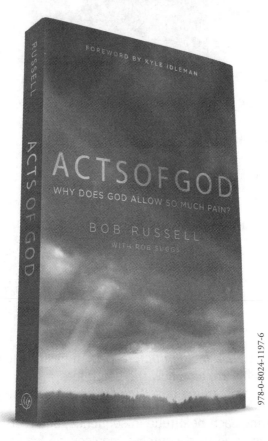

978-0-8024-1197-6

Bob Russell thinks we're asking the wrong question. Rather, we should be asking *Who?*

Who is God, and what is He doing as our hearts are hurting?

With compassion and wisdom, Bob Russell helps you turn your *Why?* into *Who?* and leads you to the God who can be trusted.

also available as an ebook

MOODY
Publishers®

From the Word to Life®